Dedications

This book is dedicated to all school counselors who touch the lives of students with special needs by endlessly giving their best to make school a positive place to grow and learn.

To my son, Brenden, my brother, and my father, who are never surprised by my ideas and who offer endless support while the ideas grow; and to my friends, who supported my vision, listened to my thoughts, and offered constant encouragement.

-- B. B.

To my husband, Robin, because he provided me with his loving support throughout the writing process for this book. For my niece, Holly, and her son, Colton, who are teaching me how important this book will be in helping school counselors provide Colton with the understanding and support he will need in his life's journey.

-- P. B.

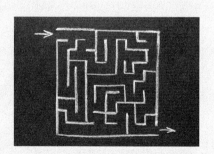

Table of Contents

About the Authors

Barbara E. Baditoi, a retired Director of Special Education and Student Services, has over 29 years of building and districtwide experience in public education. She was the first ED teacher hired in Fairfax County Public Schools, Virginia, and has professional experience as a K-12 ED/LD teacher, high school special education department chair, autism resource teacher, behavior specialist, and assistant principal.

Currently an adjunct professor of graduate education courses at Marymount University, she also supervises student teachers, and is an international educational consultant. She is the author of *When Behavior Makes Learning Hard: Positive Steps for Changing Student Behavior* (2010). Her experience and years in education have provided her with a historical and unique perspective on engaging students with special needs.

Pamelia E. Brott has 39 years of professional experience in educational settings that include being a teacher, coach, and school counselor; currently, she is a counselor educator at Virginia Tech's Northern Virginia Center in Falls Church. Dr. Brott is a National Certified Counselor, a Licensed Professional Counselor in Michigan, and a certified teacher and school counselor.

Dr. Brott is the author of 29 publications, including book chapters and professional journal articles, and is a former editor of *Professional School Counseling*. She frequently presents at state, regional, national, and international counseling conferences covering topics related to school counseling, accountability in counselor training and practice, professional identity development, and career development and counseling.

Preface

For many years, a parallel relationship existed among certified school personnel. General education teachers were in the classrooms, and special education teachers were responsible for a wide range of services for students receiving special education supports. Social workers provided case management to students and families dealing with psychosocial issues. School counselors dealt with problem behaviors, life skills, and career planning. School psychologists handled student testing for disabilities and learning problems. School nurses dispensed prescribed medications and tended to health issues. Administrators were building managers. All too often, collaboration among these highly qualified professionals on behalf of the child occurred infrequently or on an as-needed basis. Fortunately, at present there is a general realization throughout the education field that closer interaction and communication among these professionals through interprofessional collaboration and teaming is critical to meeting the needs of every student, particularly given the mandates of current federal legislation.

With burgeoning caseloads, an increasing number of students identified for special education services, and reductions in staff, many school counselors feel overwhelmed, underprepared, and in need of direction to organize their programs and practices in the schools. The purpose of this book is to provide a resource for the school counselor's professional library that will fill in the knowledge gaps and provide an understanding and framework for special education. It offers tools and helpful suggestions for developing and delivering a school counseling program that meets the needs of students with disabilities. The primary focus is a collaborative consultation approach that is based on the specialized training and expertise of a number of professionals in the schools and community support services. Each chapter begins with a Venn diagram reflecting the overlapping nature of the two complementary professions, and ends with reflective questions to assist the reader in thinking about professional practice and providing services to all students. Each chapter highlights tips, reminders, tools, and resources for teaming and collaboration.

Complementary **Professions**

Recent Trends and Current Issues

Special Education Services

- Movement from the separation of students with disabilities to inclusion in general education settings

- Impact of federal legislation and court decisions

- Evolving approaches to identifying the need for and providing special education services

- Collaborative consultation
- Advocacy
- Inclusion
- Transitions
- Accountability

Role of the School Counselor

- From directive approach to program-centered services

- Changing duties and responsibilities

- Impact of legislative and education initiatives

A Shared Vision of Special Education and School Counseling

Every day elementary and secondary public schools face the challenge and vital task of educating students. School counselors are important team members in supporting the academic achievement of every student in the school. Through the doors of these buildings walk diverse groups of students who are the heart and soul of America's future; they are varied ethnically, culturally, and in their academic strengths and challenges. School counselors take an active role in providing collaborative services to meet the needs of all students, including those with disabilities.

Approximately 13 in every 100 students in the United States receive special education services in public schools. In 2007–2008, 13.4% of the total public school enrollment, over six million students, was served under the Individuals With Disabilities Education Act (IDEA; National Center for Education Statistics, 2010). Although students with disabilities receive services through special education, school counselors are involved in many aspects of a student's academic life such as interfacing with other specialists as part of a student's individualized education program (IEP) team, helping coordinate accommodations under Section 504 Plans, providing counseling services mandated through the IEP, or attending high school transition IEP meetings to discuss possible career paths. Eligibility for special education services provides specialized instruction and accommodations; it also means the school counselor might be involved on many different levels. In the current school milieu, a school counselor's caseload continues to grow and to be more diverse and more challenging, and requires skills not always acquired through academic training.

The American School Counselor Association's (ASCA) position statement *The Professional School Counselor and Students With Special Needs* (2010b) articulates that school counselors help "all students realize their potential, and make adequate yearly progress regardless of challenges that may result from disabilities and other special needs" (¶1). Although many individuals enter the school counseling profession with inadequate knowledge and skills to meet the diverse needs that are present in schools, because of their unique training in providing a comprehensive, preventative program that is developmental in nature, school counselors are able to collaborate with others as part of a student support team to identify needs, provide services, and refer to appropriate resources both within and outside of the school (ASCA, 2005a)

The majority of the school counselor's time is to be spent in direct service to all students, including students with disabilities, although few professional school counselors feel prepared to meet the needs of this population (McEachern, 2003; Milsom, 2002). However, all students belong to all educators. The school counselor remains a vital part of a student's life, even when a student is found eligible for special education and substantial instructional responsibility shifts to special educators.

As professional duties for counselors have expanded, the counselor's role in supporting students with special needs has also evolved. The role of the counselor mirrors the changes in special education; this change signals a continuing redefinition of the role itself and of school counselors' responsibilities. Understanding the growth and development of special education and school counseling can assist in formulating a collaborative teaming approach that taps into the unique skills and training of these highly qualified school personnel. Historical events, legislation, and current trends highlight the growth and development of special education and school counseling in the United States.

Growth and Development of Special Education

It is hard to imagine that the concepts of a free and appropriate public education (FAPE), the least restrictive environment (LRE), and inclusion are relatively new. The roots of special education reflect those of the civil rights movement and have their historical beginnings in a part of U.S. history that may best be viewed with a healthy sense of discomfort and a future resolve that the past not be repeated.

In the late 19th and early 20th century, people with disabilities were institutionalized and hidden from society, often against their will. In Massachusetts, in 1893, a student with disabilities was excluded from school because "he was so weak in mind as to not derive a marked benefit from instruction, was troublesome to other children, and was unable to take ordinary, decent, physical care of himself" (*Watson v. City of Cambridge*, 1893, as cited in Yell, Rogers, & Rogers, 1998, ¶3). The eugenics movement not so subtly decreed that students with disabilities were undesirable; in 1927, the Supreme Court upheld a Virginia statute allowing forced sterilization of "mental defectives" (*Buck v. Bell;* see Dorr, 2010). Students with disabilities were either not educated and excluded from school or segregated in separate facilities. Even though by 1918 all states required compulsory education, states continued to enact statutes that allowed school officials to exclude students with disabilities—a practice that proved hard to eradicate.

There were exceptions. Samuel Gridley Howe (1801–1876), a social reformer and a graduate of Harvard Medical School, founded the Perkins School for the Blind in Boston in 1856. Thomas Gallaudet (1787–1851), a teacher of deaf and blind students, recognized the abilities of deaf students and founded a school for the deaf in Hartford, Connecticut, in 1816. In the early 20th century, Elizabeth Farrell, a teacher in New York City, began advocating for students with special needs. Along with other educators and students at Teachers College, Columbia University in New York City, Farrell founded the Council for Exceptional Children (CEC) in 1922. This major professional organization for teachers, administrators, parents, and other advocates continues to be in the forefront of advocating for children with disabilities. Psychologists became interested in the testing of children, and, in the early 20th century, professionals such as doctors and social workers became aware of the lack of services for students with disabilities.

Parents also proved to be strong advocates for their children. Yell and colleagues (1998) stated, "In response to the deplorable conditions that their children with special needs had to endure in school, as well as the increasing exclusion of children with disabilities from school, parents began to band together"(¶16). Parents and advocacy groups helped spur a growing recognition of public education's responsibility to children with disabilities. Two advocacy groups in particular, The Association for Retarded Citizens (ARC, now simply The Arc), founded in 1950, and the Association for Children With Learning Disabilities (now the Learning Disability Association of America (LDA), founded in 1964, advocated for the right to an education for students with disabilities. Although, as Hallahan and Kauffman (2006) observed, "Effective national parent organizations have existed in the United States only since 1950" (p. 26), these parent groups have been effective in providing three main functions: (a) an informal support group for parents, (b) information regarding services and resources, and (c) a structure for obtaining services for their children. Today, individual parents and parent support groups continue to advocate equal rights for children with disabilities.

Along with individuals and groups leading the cause of equal rights for students with disabilities, state laws requiring civil rights supported the need for services to be provided to students with disabilities. These laws, although laying a foundation for equality, were not enough to stop discrimination against those with disabilities; it required both a number of special education pieces of legislation and the intervention of the U.S. court system to make this a reality.

Landmark Court Cases

Even after compulsory education became the norm by 1918, with most states requiring at least elementary school attendance, students with disabilities were routinely excluded, although this began to be challenged by 1934 (see *Bd. of Educ. of Cleveland Heights v. State* ex rel *Goldman*, 1934). The 1954 Supreme Court ruling in the school desegregation case *Brown v. Board of Education* formalized the goal of equal educational opportunity and access. With this case, "the courts began to reaffirm the rights of minority citizens in a wide variety of settings" (Kirk, Gallagher, Coleman, & Anastasiow, 2009, p. 65). *Brown v. Board of Education* remains the cornerstone for disability rights even though the rights of people with disabilities continue to require the force of the law to compel changes. *Brown* became a catalyst for the American Civil Rights Movement (1955–1968), and the backbone of future rulings that students with disabilities could not be discriminated against in public schools.

The 14th Amendment to the Constitution, the basis for the *Brown* decision (1954), guaranteed equal protection under the law (and thus equal access to education for all students). The ruling in *Pennsylvania Association for Retarded Children (PARC) v. Commonwealth of Pennsylvania* (1972), a class action suit against the state of Pennsylvania, recognized that students were still unlawfully being barred from public school and set the stage for "mainstreaming," or educating students with disabilities in their neighborhood schools. In the same year, *Mills v. Board of Education of the District of Columbia* mandated that students with disabilities were entitled to a public school education and to special education services as needed. Although it appeared that American society was on the path toward celebrating diversity, states continued to deny educational access. In 1969, the State of North Carolina made it a crime for parents to challenge a decision that labeled their child as "uneducable," and therefore excluded from public school (Weber, 1992, as cited in Yell et al., 1998), and the Code of Virginia of 1973 allowed schools to exclude "children physically or mentally incapacitated for school work" (Mastropieri & Scruggs, 2004, p. 6).

Among the landmark court cases strengthening the rights of students with disabilities was the Supreme Court's decision in *Hudson v. Rowley* (1982), a ruling that FAPE does not mean that students must attain the maximum possible achievement, but ensures that they must be making progress. This ruling established the base for providing special education services in what has come to be called the "*Rowley* standard": The primary purpose of special education is to provide access, and the IEP must be "reasonably calculated to enable the child to receive passing marks and advance from grade to grade" (*Rowley*, 458 U.S. at 206–07, 1982).

MANIFEST DETERMINATION

Honig v. Doe (1988) established that children with social and academic problems could not be excluded from school for behavior relating to their condition. Other court decisions also have maintained the rights of students with disabilities, helping to define FAPE and LRE (see Table 1.1). Kirk et al. (2009) summarized the importance of the U.S. court system: "[It] has played a significant role in the lives of exceptional children and their families . . . the rulings in several court cases have reaffirmed the rights of those who are handicapped and have defined the limits of those rights" (p. 65).

Federal Special Education Legislation

Concurrent with these judicial decisions providing an impetus for an inclusive education for students with disabilities, federal legislation formalized and legalized the educational rights of children. Table 1.2 provides a summary of federal legislation related to special education. Four acts in particular continue to impact the role of today's school counselors: the Elementary and Secondary Education Act of 1965 (ESEA; reauthorized as the No Child Left Behind Act of 2001, NCLB), the Rehabilitation Act of 1973 (Section 504), the Education for All Handicapped Children's Act of 1975 (EHA; today's IDEA), and the Americans With Disabilities Act of 1990.

Elementary and Secondary Education Act of 1965 (later known as NCLB)

With passage of ESEA in 1965, Congress promoted equal access for poor and minority students and, for the first time, provided funds to educate students with disabilities (Title I). The Act was reauthorized as the Improving America's Schools Act of 1994, passed the same year as the Goals 2000: Educate America Act. These two pieces of legislation reflected a shift in focus: Public schools would be held accountable for content and performance standards, regular assessment of students, and a means of ensuring that all students received the support they needed "to perform as expected on those assessments" (Jorgensen & Hoffmann, 2003, p. 4). By the turn of the 21st century, many states had instituted common content standards and assessments.

Table 1.1 Landmark Court Cases in Special Education

Year	Case	Ruling
1934	Board of Education of Cleveland Heights v. State	Local boards of education may not exclude students with disabilities from school.
1954	Brown v. Board of Education	Supreme Court held segregation of students by race unconstitutional; ended "separate but equal."
1972	Pennsylvania Association for Retarded Children v. Commonwealth of Pennsylvania	Students with mental retardation are guaranteed the right to an education.
1972	Mills v. Board of Education	Children with exceptionalities are entitled to a public education regardless of their functional level.
1982	Board of Education of Hendrick Hudson Central School District v. Rowley	Supreme Court ruling that an appropriate education does not necessarily mean an education that allows for the maximum achievement, but rather a reasonable opportunity to learn.
1982	Oberti v. Board of Education	Clarified the concept of least restrictive environment: Placement in general education classroom with supplementary aids and services must be offered prior to considering more segregated placements.
1984	Irving Independent School District v. Tatro	Supreme Court ruled that under special education laws, schools must provide related services as needed by the student to receive a free, appropriate public education.
1988	Honig v. Doe	Supreme Court ruling that students with social and academic problems could not be excluded from school for behavior related to their disability.
2005	Schaeffer v. Weast	Supreme Court ruled that the party seeking relief bears the burden of proof in a due process hearing.

Table 1.2   Federal Legislation Related to Special Education

Year	Events	Counseling Focus
1958	Education of Mentally Retarded Children Act (Pub. L. 94-142)	Provided assistance for training teachers of students with mental retardation.
1963	Community Mental Health Act (Pub. L. 88-164)	Provided funding for professionals to receive training to work with students with disabilities.
1965	Elementary and Secondary Education Act (Pub. L. 89-10)	Legislated equal access for poor and minority children and funding for services for students with disabilities.
1973	Rehabilitation Act (Pub. L. 93-112)	Section 504 established rights of qualified individuals with disabilities to equal access to federally funded programs and businesses.
1975	Education for All Handicapped Children's Act (EHA; Pub. L. 94-142)	Established a free and appropriate public education (FAPE) in the least restricted environment (LRE) and mandated that FAPE be available to all handicapped students; provided federal funding to states to assist in educating students with disabilities.
1983	EHA Amendments (Pub. L. 98-198)	Addressed transition through research and development of model transition programs.
1986	EHA Amendments (Pub. L. 99-457)	Mandated comprehensive services for early childhood (birth to age 3) and expanded services for preschool children.
1990	Americans With Disabilities Act (Pub. L. 101-336)	Focused on eliminating discrimination against individuals with disabilities in specific industries and government-funded operations.
1990	Individuals With Disabilities Education Act (Pub. L. 101-336)	Replaced the term handicapped with disabled and added transition planning requirement, and added autism and TBI to disability list.
1997	Amendments to the IDEA (Pub. L. 105-17)	Mandated state- and districtwide assessments and positive behavior supports based on functional behavior assessment and behavior intervention plans. Also added ADHD to the disability list.
2000	Goals 2000: Educate America Act (Pub. L. 103-227)	Directed states to establish programs for increasing partnerships with families, specifically including parents of children with disabilities.
2001	No Child Left Behind Act (Pub. L. 107-110)	Established an accountability system for states based on annual yearly testing for all students.
2004	Individuals With Disabilities Education Improvement Act (Pub. L. 108-446)	Established the option of using a response to intervention model (aka research-based intervention) for the identification of students with learning disabilities.

Note: TBI - traumatic brain injury; ADHD = attention deficit hyperactivity disorder.

In 2001, ESEA's reauthorization as NCLB expanded the federal role in education. NCLB expected that all students (including those with disabilities) would participate and progress in the general education curriculum, and achieve and be assessed at a level equal to their typically developing peers. Because NCLB held states accountable for all students, and data were to be disaggregated for students with disabilities, school districts needed to provide all students with the same state-mandated curriculum and assessments, unless the student's IEP deemed an alternative assessment was appropriate. Indeed, one of the foundations of NCLB was to ensure that students with disabilities would not be "left behind" in making progress toward their academic goals. The forward motion of the reading and math goals requires continuous accountability of all states, school divisions, and schools to achieve adequate yearly progress (AYP) and monitoring of academic achievement.

NCLB has had a major impact on educational staff. Although not specifically delivering academic instruction, school counselors work with students and collaborate and support teachers who may feel increased pressure for students to perform well on state-mandated exams. This effectively raises the profile of school counselors, requiring them to be an ongoing part of schoolwide assessment and evaluation, while at the same time sustaining those affected by the implementation of the Act.

Education for All Handicapped Children's Act of 1975 (IDEA)

EHA (1975) introduced the concept of FAPE in the least restrictive environment appropriate, for all children with disabilities—at a time when approximately one million students were still excluded from attending public school (National Council on Disability, 2000), especially those with hearing or vision impairments, emotional disorders, or intellectual disabilities. EHA mandated due process rights and parent participation, and strengthened the requirement for a written IEP, although special education students were still excluded from state testing. It also mandated that students with disabilities had a right to nondiscriminatory testing, evaluation, and placement procedures. EHA "expanded the school counselors' roles into special education, including appropriate placement services, collaboration in the individual education plan process, record-keeping management, and providing consultation and counseling service to children with disabilities, their parents and/or guardians, and their teachers" (Humes, 1978, as cited in Lambie & Williamson, 2004, p. 126).

Reauthorization of EHA in 1986 added a requirement that infants and toddlers must be provided with Child Find Early Intervention Services, to guarantee that young children with disabilities would be identified at an early age. In 1990 Congress renamed EHA the Individuals With Disabilities Education Act; in addition to eliminating the use of the term *handicapped*, this reauthorization added detailed transition planning by the age of 16, and added two more categories to the list of federally defined areas of disability: traumatic brain injury (TBI) and autism. Students were to be educated in public schools, although in reality they were often segregated in self-contained classes or educated in separate buildings.

In its 1997 reauthorization of IDEA, Congress added attention deficit hyperactivity disorder as an "other health impairment," and required functional behavior assessments and behavior intervention plans to assist professional staff in supporting students with challenging behaviors. This reauthorization mandated state- and districtwide assessments for all students, and required that a student's IEP include measurable goals that provide educators and parents with a method for determining individual progress. Instead of focusing on *where* students with disabilities should be educated, "the new focus defined this in terms of their access to the general education curriculum" (Zigmond, 2003, p. 194). Congress also encouraged school boards and parents to resolve their differences through nonadversarial means such as mediation.

Of special importance to school counselors were regulations that broadened the scope of related services offered to students with disabilities; these services would assist the student to benefit from special education and included psychological services, counseling services, and parent counseling and training (IDEA, 2006, Part 300.24[b]). This regulation was further clarified; "Counseling services means services provided by qualified social workers, psychologist, guidance counselors, or other qualified personnel" (Part 300.24[b][2]). Thus, both special education students (through their IEP) and their parents could be provided with counseling services to assist students in making educational progress.

Regulations accompanying this new IDEA also discussed the use of positive behavior support (PBS), with an "emphasis on using functional assessment and positive approaches to encourage good behavior" (Office of Special Education Programs, n.d.-a, ¶1). Congress stopped short of mandating implementation of PBS, strongly encouraging it as a method of promoting behavioral supports on a schoolwide basis. This approach, the only one mentioned specifically in the law, has become more prevalent in succeeding years, bringing with it the requirement that educational personnel, including school counselors, are aware of this method of behavior support (see Chapter 5).

In reauthorizing IDEA in 2004 as the Individuals With Disabilities Education Improvement Act, Congress acknowledged the impact of other education legislation and focused on improving outcomes for students with disabilities by

- emphasizing the substantive requirements of the special education process;

- aligning IDEA with NCLB's provisions such as adequate yearly progress (AYP), highly qualified personnel, and evidence-based practices; and

- altering eligibility requirements. (Yell, Shriner, & Katsiyannis, 2006, p. 2)

The increasing attention and use of response-to-intervention (RTI) strategies in identifying the need for and providing special education services was also reflected in this most recent reauthorization. The IDEA legislation and regulations do not specifically refer to RTI, but rather indicate a preference for "research-based methods" of evaluating a student's need for special education services (rather than a discrepancy between IQ and achievement); the original language requiring research-based methods for identification and servicing was softened a bit to give states a choice in practice. This change, however, gave states more discretion in determining how students with learning differences are identified, and in using interventions in the general education setting prior to identifying students for special education. Figure 1.1 presents evolving depictions of the three-tiered RTI framework. The original pyramid graphic provided an illustration of RTI implementation based on a schoolwide model; the second illustrated the incorporation of Positive Behavioral Interventions and Supports (PBIS), showing that the RTI framework incorporated effective instructional strategies for both academic and behavior systems. The circle graphic is the current model of RTI as a continuous process. Chapter 3 contains more information about the concept of RTI and the role of school counselors.

Section 504 of the Rehabilitation Act of 1973 and the Americans With Disabilities Act (ADA)

The Rehabilitation Act of 1973, a broad antidiscrimination act, mandated that public institutions that received federal monies (such as public schools) could not discriminate against people with disabilities. Section 504 specifically addresses access to public programs and services. Because school counselors can be case managers for students with Section 504 Plans, they need to be up to date on both the regulations governing eligibility for such plans and appropriate classroom accommodations.

The Americans With Disabilities Act (ADA, 2006) ensured the right of individuals with disabilities to nondiscriminatory practices and equal opportunities in the workplace, transportation, state and local government, public access, and telecommunications. This impacted public schools because, as recipients of federal funds, schools were required to guarantee accommodations. In 2008, the Americans With Disabilities Act Amendments Act (ADAAA, 2009) broadened the parameters of the original ADA, expanded the definition of what type of impairments require accommodations, denied the need for mitigating circumstances (except for glasses), and generally promoted the idea that ADA of 1990 was too narrow in its definition and application. ADAAA included a "conforming amendment" to Section 504 of the Rehabilitation Act, meaning that the newly expanded coverage under ADAAA also applied to Section 504. It is essential that school counselors understand the legal changes to the law; Chapter 7 is devoted to a comprehensive explanation of the roots of the ADA and the impact of ADAAA on Section 504 Plans.

Current Federal Support for Special Education

Although both the courts and Congress have steadily promoted the rights of persons with disabilities, monetary assistance by the federal government for the costs of providing an education for students with disabilities has never followed suit. IDEA 2004 enacted certain regulations for states to follow, but the federal government did not support the additions to the law with monetary support; "the new IDEA's financial provisions offer[ed] little relief for the cost of special education" (CEC, 2010, ¶3). Instead of mandating full funding, IDEA 2004 maintained then-current funding levels and suggested the federal government would pay "40 percent of the excess cost of educating students with disabilities by 2010" (CEC, 2010, ¶3).

In 2009, in an effort to boost a sagging economy, Congress passed the American Recovery and Reinvestment Act of 2009 (ARRA), a measure targeted to pump money into the economy, including health, education and social services programs. ARRA provided additional funding for states to spend on special education over 2 years. Although $12.2 billion was targeted for IDEA special education services—a number not close to the actual funding needed—partial federal monetary participation has increased. However, because the stimulus package was a one-time funding source, increased federal support for special education will probably remain only partially funded.

The U.S. Department of Education's "Race to the Top" grant competition in 2010 provided additional federal aid for education; funds were tied to specific criteria such as "adopting internationally benchmarked standards, improving the recruitment, retention, and rewarding of educators, improving data collection, and turning around the lowest-performing schools" (McNeil, 2009, ¶12). Grants to improve education continue to be awarded; clearly, any increased or new funding will require additional assessment and accountability, impacting all school personnel—including the school counselor.

Figure 1.1 The Evolution of RTI

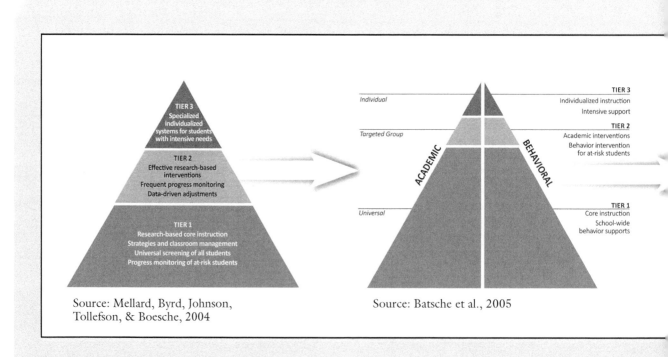

Source: Mellard, Byrd, Johnson, Tollefson, & Boesche, 2004

Source: Batsche et al., 2005

Growth and Development of School Counseling

School counseling has evolved from a directive approach focused on moral and vocational guidance in the late 1800s to the 21st century's program-centered services based on national standards and a model that focuses on supporting the academic success of all students. The history of school counseling can be seen as a series of reactions to social, political, and economic conditions, and to federal legislation. Although school counseling has been rooted in career guidance from its inception, over the past hundred-plus years school counselors have taken on an ever-increasing level of roles and responsibilities while relinquishing few of their assigned duties (see Figure 1.2).

Principals continue to have a significant influence on the roles and responsibilities of school counselors (Chata & Loesch, 2007). Previous research has shown that many principals expect school counselors to register new students, administer tests, and maintain student records, all of which are basically clerical tasks (Pérusse, Goodnough, Donegan, & Jones, 2004). This has left many school counselors feeling overwhelmed and underappreciated in their professional role. However, the transformed school counselor of the 21st century with support from the principal provides a comprehensive program consisting

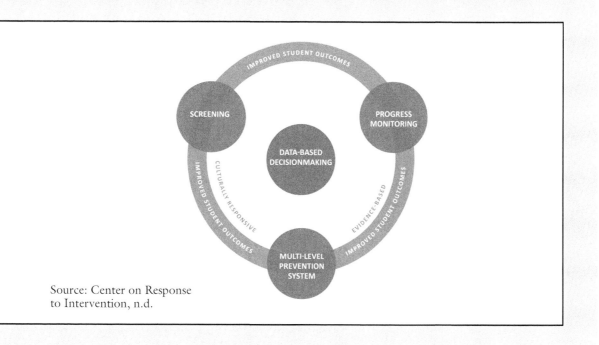

Source: Center on Response to Intervention, n.d.

Figure 1.2 School Counselors' Roles and Responsibilities

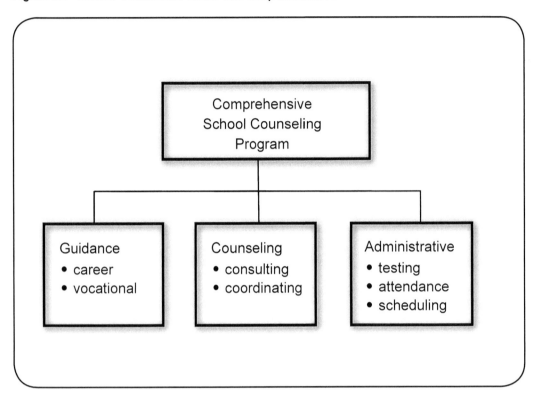

of a foundation, delivery of services, management of the program, and account-ability (see ASCA 2005a). This program is built on a foundation of beliefs and standards for the academic, career, and personal/social development needs of students. The delivery of services includes counseling, guiding, consulting, and collaborating. Managing the program focuses attention on informing all stakeholders, including principals, of the school counselor's scope of respon-sibility. Accountability is the key in providing evidence-based practice that the services provided are meeting the needs of the school population.

A myriad of needs continue to impact the school counseling program. As discussed previously, legislation and education initiatives have brought to the forefront issues related to multicultural and special needs of increasingly diverse populations in the schools. This necessitates that school counselors be trained to identify and meet these needs. The impact of geography and setting (urban, suburban, rural), socioeconomic status, race, ethnicity, gender, and disability are important considerations for the transformed school counselor.

To better understand the current function of school counseling, a review of the historical growth and development of the profession helps to place the relationship of school counseling to special education in context and to explain the varied duties assigned to school counselors in the 21st century. Figure 1.3 provides a summary of significant events and legislation that have impacted the role of school counselors.

The Beginnings of School Counseling

Guidance and counseling in schools is an American invention (Erford, 2007). The earliest recorded practices giving rise to school counseling were rooted in vocational guidance:

- Lysander Richards, who called for a new profession of vocational assistance in 1881;

- George Merrill's vocational guidance practice in the 1890s;

- Eli W. Weaver's New York City schools peer advising program (1904);

- Jesse B. Davis's 1908 vocational and moral guidance program; and

- the founding of the Vocations Bureau of Boston in 1908 and publication of *Choosing a Vocation*, both the work of Frank Parsons (Erford, 2007; Savickas, 2009).

These practices are reflective of changes in the United States marked by industrialization, influx of immigrants, and migration of Americans into urban areas.

In the early 20th century, federal legislation supported providing vocational education in the public schools. The Smith-Hughes Act of 1917, also known as the Vocational Education Act, gave more responsibility to the states and localities to prepare students for employment. Careers that previously had required on-the-job-training now moved to vocational training in the public schools. The George-Reed Act of 1919 subsidized vocational education and teacher training. This legislation emphasizing vocational guidance gave rise to the need for standardized measures.

The psychometric movement grew out of scientific methods with applications in schools and in the military. The use of mental ability measurements (i.e., intelligence testing) to classify students for educational instruction popularized the use of psychometric principles to solve practical problems. With the entry of the United States into World War I in 1917, the military successfully developed achievement tests that could be administered to groups and be used to classify men eligible to serve. The Army Alpha, a paper-and-pencil test, and Army Beta, a nonverbal intelligence test, were the forerunners of the current Armed Services Vocational Aptitude Battery (ASVAB). The success of group testing in the military influenced the development of standardized tests for college admissions, such as the American College Test (ACT) and Scholastic Assessment Test (SAT), both still prevalent today.

During the 1920s and 1930s, emphasis in the schools was centered on compulsory school attendance, selection of courses, and postsecondary pursuits (whether vocational or college). In many high schools, school counselors acquired various administrative responsibilities related to student discipline, attendance, and guidance. State guidance directors were appointed to develop and coordinate testing programs in the schools, with local test administration usually being handled by the school counselor. It was at this time that the term *counseling* rather than *guidance* began to be used.

Figure 1.3   Chronological Overview of School Counseling Focus

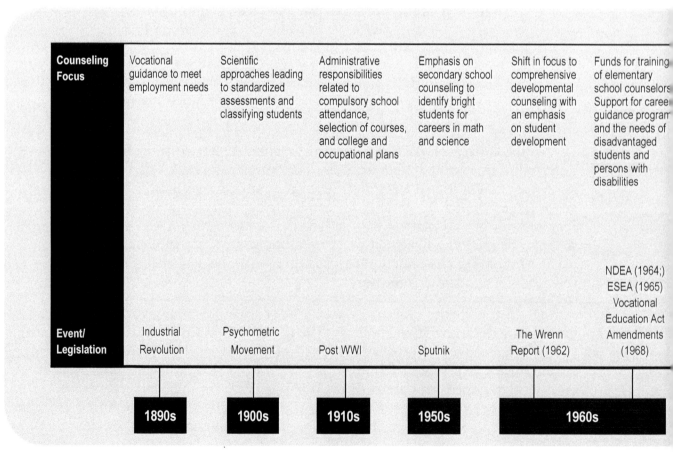

Directive Approach to School Counseling

The directive approach to counseling, generally based on Frank Parson's approach to vocational guidance, employs testing in the assessment phase, increasing knowledge through the information phase, and guidance in making decisions for the placement phase (Savickas, 2009). This model placed the counselor in an authoritative role and was directive or "counselor-centered" with a relatively narrow focus on vocational guidance and administrative duties. This approach dominated the field into the 1940s when Carl Rogers introduced a more "person-centered" approach to counseling.

The launching of Sputnik in 1957 sparked the rapid development of secondary school counseling. The perceived threat of Soviet supremacy fueled passage of the National Defense Education Act (NDEA) of 1958, which provided funds for the enhancement of school counseling programs and the preparation of school counselors—with the ultimate goal of identifying bright

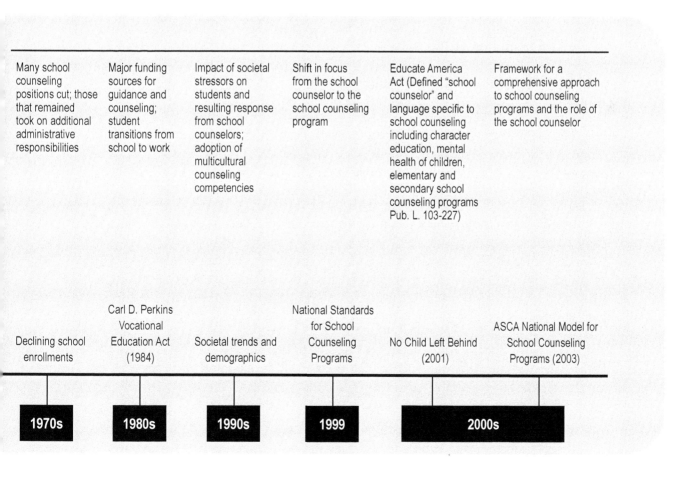

students for careers in math and science. The role of the school counselor was to identify these students (assessment and testing), place them in math and science courses (placement), and guide them to attend college (guidance). Many of the school counselor's duties were administrative and clerical rather than counseling to meet the needs of testing, placement, and guidance. During this time the training of school counselors consisted of four or five university courses that were required for state certification and, in most states, classroom teaching experience was required. Many school counselors viewed their position as a stepping-stone to becoming a principal and, therefore, embraced their administrative role in the schools.

Comprehensive Developmental School Counseling

The next shift in school counseling, a trend toward providing counseling services to all students from elementary through high school, was initiated with the 1962 publication of the Wrenn report, *The Counselor in a Changing World*. The report was a result of the Commission on Guidance established by the American Personnel and Guidance Association (APGA) to (a) study the role and function of school counselors, (b) review the preparation of school counselors, and (c) make recommendations for school counseling. These recommendations included individual and group counseling to students; consultation to parents and teachers; and an emphasis on student developmental needs that included personal growth, self-determination, and self-responsibility. The published findings prompted a movement away from directive guidance for selected students and towards a developmental preventative counseling approach for all students.

The NDEA amendments of 1964 supported the development and training of elementary school counselors. ESEA (Titles I and III) provided support for elementary school counseling, further supporting school counseling programs to become comprehensive (K–12) and developmentally appropriate.

Funds through the Vocational Education Act Amendments of 1968 supported career guidance programs at both the elementary and secondary levels providing further interest in comprehensive services. These amendments also responded to the needs of disadvantaged students and people with disabilities, for the first time specifically linking school counseling to supporting students with disabilities.

Following the passage of EHA and its introduction of the concept of FAPE for students who needed special education and related services due to an eligible disability, school counselors started to assume the role of referring students with disabilities to those trained to serve this population, such as special educators and school psychologists (Scarborough & Gilbride, 2006). Some counselors also assisted in developing student IEPs, even acting as case managers. School counselors began to devote significant time to handling paperwork and attending meetings. However, some school counselors embraced this legislation as an opportunity to become more involved in providing counseling services to students with disabilities and to their families.

It was at this point that school counseling services were provided to all students from elementary through high school. This shift was reflected in what was commonly referred to as *comprehensive developmental school counseling programs* and is used to this day to describe school counseling programs.

This period in American history saw increasing unemployment and declining school enrollments. In many instances, reductions in school personnel meant cutting school counseling positions. To protect their jobs, some school counselors assumed additional responsibilities, many of which were administrative and "noncounseling" activities.

Still, there continued to be an emphasis on career guidance. The Carl D. Perkins Vocational Education Act of 1984 (now known as Perkins IV) has been a major funding source for guidance and counseling in the schools since the 1980s, which includes services for students with disabilities. With the 1994 School to Work Opportunities Act, secondary school counselors were called on to deliver career guidance and counseling services that supported students transitioning from school to work, again including students with disabilities.

Impact of Societal Stressors on School Counseling

The final decades of the 20th century brought a variety of societal stressors to the forefront in American schools. These stressors included an increased emphasis on K-to-12 educational standards for more rigorous academics; inclusion practices for exceptional students and culturally different populations; awareness of the need to address the effects of drug abuse (and efforts to prevent drug use by students); promotion of gender equity; and effects of the changing family, such as divorce and dual careers of parents (Baker & Gerler, 2008). Because of the impact on school-age students, school counselors needed to take on additional responsibilities. Multiculturalism was introduced as the "fourth force" in counseling, and was the focus of a special issue of the premier counseling journal *Journal of Counseling & Development*. The Association for Multicultural Counseling and Development established multicultural counseling competencies and standards. The *National Standards for*

School Counseling Programs (Campbell & Dahir, 1997) shifted the focus from the school counselor to the school counseling program, created a program framework, linked the program to the academic mission of education, provided equal access for all students from a developmental perspective with identified student knowledge and skills, and stressed that the school counseling program be comprehensive and systemic in the delivery of services.

Development and Transformation as a Profession

In 1913, Jesse B. Davis helped form the first professional association known as the National Vocational Guidance Association (NVGA). NVGA, the American College Personnel Association, the National Association of Guidance Supervisors and Counselor Trainers, and the Student Personnel Association for Teacher Education merged in 1951 to form American Personnel and Guidance Association (APGA). Over the years, the name changed from the APGA to the American Counseling Association (ACA). The American School Counselor Association (ASCA) was instituted in 1952 and became a division of APGA in 1953.

ASCA provides "one vision and one voice" for the profession (2005a). The leadership has advocated for identifying the profession as *school counseling* and using the title *professional school counselor*. The ASCA leadership has been instrumental in standardizing the practice of professional school counseling through the ASCA National Model (2005a). The Model is a guide for designing, developing, implementing, and evaluating a school counseling program with the goal to support all students in achieving academic success. School counselors collaborate with others to ensure that the school counseling program is "comprehensive in scope, preventative in design and developmental in nature" (ASCA, 2005a, p. 13).

Professional school counseling is being transformed to meet the needs of a rapidly changing society. The demands on schools from federal legislation and economic competition in the workforce challenge counselors to become advocates for social justice and active agents in school reform. School counselors need to move out of the traditional mode of services for some students to being proactive leaders and advocates for the success of all students (Erford, 2007).

Recent Trends Impacting Complementary Professions

Federal mandates and regulations, court decisions, and congressional involvement have modified and changed the landscape for students receiving special education services. Many special education students today are educated in inclusive general education classrooms, which increases the responsibility of the general education teachers and expands the school counselor's role. Trends in special education that impact school counselors include (a) increased accountability through data reporting; (b) continuing movement towards full inclusion; (c) assistance with transitions; (d) intensification of collaboration and teaming; (e) behavior management; and (f) legislation. These myriad areas rest on a comprehensive knowledge of best practices and an understanding of current legislation and regulations (see Figure 1.4).

Although school counselors may not be directly responsible for the stream of data now required by state and local school divisions, the collection of such information filters down to the professionals working at a school-based level. For the school counselor, this means that interventions are supported with evidence that shows best practices are working for students. Although **accountability** is the key in providing evidence that the services are meeting the needs of the school population, increased demands with less funding and less support put the school counselor in the position of meeting accountability requirements with fewer resources.

The second trend impacting counselors is the practice of **inclusion**. Initial attempts to place special education students in general education classrooms was called *mainstreaming*, which emphasized that students with disabilities had to "earn" their way into the LRE. This depicted "an attitude that students with disabilities really belong to special education and that they only visit the general education classroom" (Mastropieri & Scruggs, 2004, p. 7). With IDEA, however, this approach changed: In our current educational milieu, "inclusive schools do not require that students be ready to fit into the established educational programs as mainstreaming did" (Bradley, King-Sears, & Tessier-Switlick, 1997, p. 6). Heterogeneous classrooms support the needs of all students and welcome students with or without disabilities. Today, more students are educated in the general education classroom, considered the LRE for many students with disabilities. School counselors serve a vital role in advocating for students and parents and collaborating with general and special education teachers to promote inclusive best practices.

Another trend resulting in school counselors assuming a more crucial role within the school team is their participation in developing **postsecondary transition plans** for students with IEPs. Chapter 6 explains in detail how school counselors participate in the transition activities of special education students at all grade levels but particularly during the transition from middle school to high school and from high school to beyond.

Figure 1.4 Trends: School Counselors in the Center of Change

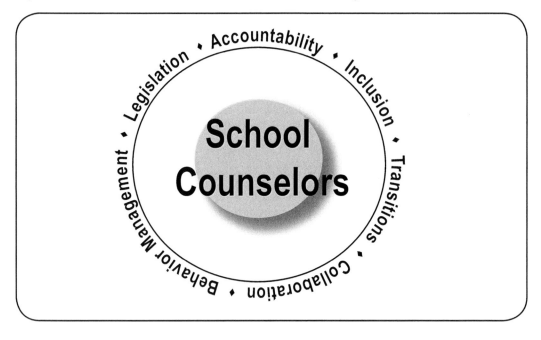

Collaboration and teaming requires the valuable input of the school counselor. Student assistance teams, RTI, and the special education eligibility and IEP process increase the responsibilities of the school counselor as a part of school teams. Collaboration and cooperation is explored in more depth in Chapter 3, along with the different roles the school counselor might assume in special education.

Another trend that influences the role of the school counselor is how to respond to students who exhibit behaviors that impact both school routine and academic achievement. School personnel remain challenged by students with difficult behavior. School counselors often step in to provide guidance and make suggestions for working with students whose behavior may interfere with their learning. Chapter 5 is devoted to a comprehensive discussion of the role of the school counselor in **behavior management**.

Finally, counselors need to be aware of the development and implementation of various changes in **legislation**, including the provision of counseling services (Chapter 4), students who receive services under Section 504 (Chapter 7), and the implications of confidentiality and privacy (Chapter 8).

Summary

Based on the growth and development of these complementary professions, there exists a shared vision of special education and school counseling. School counselors support students with disabilities through providing advocacy, supporting inclusion, embracing accountability, participating in evidence-based practices, and focusing on transitions. School counselors have specific responsibilities in order to demonstrate this shared vision for all students, including those with disabilities, and to ensure that all students have access to the school counseling program (ASCA, 2010b; see Table 1.3).

Chapter 2 provides suggestions for how the transformed school counselor can develop and implement a comprehensive program that meets the needs of every student including students with disabilities. The ASCA National Model (2005a) is used as the organizing structure for the program.

Reflective Questions

- What are the implications of the history of special education for a public school counselor?

- How does the development of school counseling interface with that of special education?

Table 1.3   Supporting Students With Disabilities Through the School Counseling Program

Do You Do This?

1. Advocate for students with disabilities in the school and in the community.

2. Ensure the activities in the comprehensive school counseling program address the needs of students with disabilities.

3. Collaborate with other school personnel (e.g., special education teachers, school psychologists, school social workers, nurses, administrators) to determine the needs and evaluate the effectiveness of services for students with disabilities.

4. Provide responsive services (e.g., individual and group counseling, assist with behavior modification plans, individual student planning, transition services) to students with disabilities and their families.

5. Serve as a consultant to parents/guardians to help them better understand the special needs of students with disabilities.

6. Consult with community professionals (e.g., social workers, therapists, doctors) regarding special needs for students with disabilities.

The School Counseling Program

Foundations for the Transformed School Counseling Program

Special Education Services

- Specialized approaches to meeting the academic, social and behavioral needs of students with disabilities
- Impact of federal legislation
- Expertise in identifying and supporting students with disabilities in various education settings

- Collaborative consultation
- Advocacy
- Inclusion
- Transitions
- Accountability

Role of the School Counselor

- Developmental in nature
- Follow identified standards for academic, career, and personal/social domains
- Ethical practices advocacy leadership

A Shared Vision of Special Education and School Counseling

The ASCA National Model for School Counseling Programs (ASCA Model; 2005a; see Figure 2.1) is a framework for providing a comprehensive approach to school counseling and organizing the program components of foundation, delivery system, management system, and accountability:

Foundation:

The beliefs and philosophy of all personnel involved in the program. The developmental domains of academic, career, and personal/social support the learning process. Student competencies in these developmental domains are articulated through national (ASCA National Standards; Campbell & Dahir, 1997), state, or local standards for school counseling programs.

Delivery System:

A comprehensive program is implemented through the guidance curriculum, individual student planning, responsive services, and system support. Support includes professional development, consultation, collaboration and teaming, and operation of the program.

Management System:

The program is managed through agreements, data, and action plans. Management agreements between school counselors and administrators ensure an understanding for the school counselor's scope of responsibility. Data-driven decisions are based on student outcomes and guide school counselors to determine ways of closing the gap (i.e., where you are, where you want to be, how to get there). A plan of action is devised for activities, use of time, and weekly/monthly/yearly calendars.

Accountability:

The evidence that the program is making a difference. The program audit, results reports, and evaluation of school counselors based on performance standards provide evidence of accountability.

Figure 2.1 ASCA National Model for School Counseling Programs

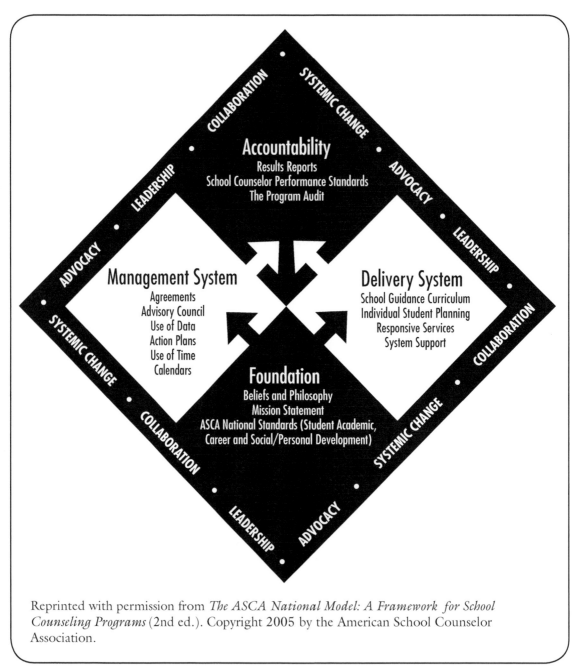

Reprinted with permission from *The ASCA National Model: A Framework for School Counseling Programs* (2nd ed.). Copyright 2005 by the American School Counselor Association.

The themes of leadership, advocacy, and collaboration are the school counselor's skills and attitudes that lead to systemic change and unite the four program components as an integrated and interdependent system.

The ASCA National Standards for Students (ASCA, 2005a) speak to specific student competencies and indicators that guide the school counselor in providing a school counseling program to meet the developmental needs (i.e., academic, career, social/emotional) of all students. The Standards describe what students should be able to do so they can achieve their highest potential in the educational setting (ASCA, 2005a). Academic, career, and personal/social domains address the importance for students to plan, develop, acquire, and apply skills that relate to school success and transitions:

Academic Development:

- Students will acquire the attitudes, knowledge and skills that contribute to effective learning in school and across the life span.

- Students will complete school with the academic preparation essential to choose from a wide range of substantial post-secondary options, including college.

- Students will understand the relationship of academics to the world of work and to life at home and in the community.

Career Development:

- Students will acquire the skills to investigate the world of work in relation to knowledge of self and to make informed career decisions.

- Students will employ strategies to achieve future career goals with success and satisfaction.

- Students will understand the relationship between personal qualities, education, training and the world of work.

Personal/Social Development:

- Students will acquire the knowledge, attitudes and interpersonal skills to help them understand and respect self and others.

- Students will make decisions, set goals and take necessary action to achieve goals.

- Students will understand safety and survival skills. (ASCA, 2005a, pp. 102–107)

The National Career Development Guidelines (National Career Development Association, NCDA, 2004) present student goals in the domains of educational achievement and lifelong learning, career management, and personal social development. Within these domains a number of goals are directly related to student success and school transitions:

Personal Social Development Domain:

- Develop understanding of self to build and maintain a positive self-concept.

- Develop positive interpersonal skills including respect for diversity.

- Integrate growth and change into your career development.

- Balance personal, leisure, community, learner, family and work roles.

Educational Achievement and Lifelong Learning Domain:

- Attain educational achievement and performance levels needed to reach your personal and career goals.

- Participate in ongoing, lifelong learning experiences to enhance your ability to function effectively in a diverse and changing economy.

Career Management Domain:

- Create and manage a career plan that meets your career goals.

- Use a process of decision-making as one component of career development.

- Use accurate, current and unbiased career information during career planning and management.

- Master academic, occupational and general employability skills in order to obtain, create, maintain and/or advance your employment.

- Integrate changing employment trends, societal needs and economic conditions into your career plans. (NCDA, 2004, ¶1–3)

The transformed school counselor is involved in leadership, advocacy, teaming and collaboration, and the use of data to ensure educational equity (ASCA, 2005a). School counselors work with resources both inside and outside of the school system to develop and deliver a comprehensive developmental school counseling program. By identifying and removing barriers, school counselors can set the tone for inclusion, particularly for students with special needs.

As discussed in Chapter 1, school counselors are critical players in facilitating the educational success for all students. School counselors use their specialized training in understanding human development and providing comprehensive school counseling programs as visible advocates and leaders in the school. School counselors must be well informed about the cultural and linguistic diversity of the school community to ensure that all students have equal access to and benefits from the school counseling program.

The Professional School Counselor

Professional school counselors are uniquely qualified through graduate training and state licensure/certification to deliver a school counseling program that addresses the academic, personal/social, and career development needs of all students (ASCA, 2009). The themes (i.e., leadership, advocacy, collaboration and teaming, systemic change) guide professional school counselors as they promote equity and access to successful educational experiences for students (ASCA, 2005b). School counselors can be found in elementary, junior/middle, and high school settings.

Most states no longer require teacher certification to become certified or licensed as a professional school counselor. The Council for the Accreditation of Counseling and Related Educational Programs (CACREP) does not identify "special education," "special needs," or "students with disabilities" as specific curricular experiences for those preparing to become school counselors (CACREP, 2009). Research on school counselor preparation in meeting the needs of students with disabilities indicates that the majority of school counselors do not feel prepared to work with students with disabilities (McEachern, 2003; Milsom, 2002). Although many individuals enter the profession with inadequate knowledge and skills to meet the needs of students with disabilities, given their training in providing a comprehensive, preventative school counseling program that is developmental in nature, school counselors can meet the needs of a diverse student population. School counselors are able to collaborate with others as part of a student support team to identify needs and, when necessary, refer to appropriate resources both within and outside of the school (ASCA, 2005a).

Today's School Counselor

Professional school counselors are advocates, leaders, collaborators and consultants who create opportunities for equity in access and success in educational opportunities by connecting their programs to the mission of schools and subscribing to the following tenets of professional responsibility: ...each person has access to a comprehensive school counseling program that advocates for and affirms all students from diverse populations including... abilities/disabilities each person has the right to receive the information and support needed to move toward self-direction and self-development and affirmation within one's group identities, with special care being given to students who have historically not received adequate educational services: ..students with disabilities... (ASCA, 2010a, Preamble).

The Professional School Counselor and Students With Special Needs

The school counselor takes an active role as a student advocate and provides collaborative services with other educational professionals to meet the needs of students with disabilities (ASCA, 2010b). ASCA (2010b) has stressed that it is inappropriate for school counselors to serve in supervisory or administrative roles. However, it is important for school counselors to understand and participate in providing support to students with disabilities. Counselors:

- participate in school multidisciplinary teams;

- collaborate in delivery special education support services;

- advocate for students with disabilities;

- assist in developing individualized education program (IEP) academic and transition plans;

- provide classroom guidance and individual and group counseling; and

- consult and collaborate with teachers, other support specialists, and parents to understand the student's unique needs (ASCA, 2010b).

Ethical Standards for School Counselors

The principles of ethical behavior for professional school counselors are delineated in the *Ethical Standards for School Counselors* (ASCA, 2010a; see Appendix B). The standards of integrity, leadership, and professionalism imbue the school counselor's responsibilities to students, parents/guardians, colleagues and professional associates, the school and community, self, and the profession. The school counselor's professional responsibility includes ensuring that all students—including those with disabilities—have access to the school counseling program and the information and support needed to move toward self-direction and self-development. Professional school counselors should (a) acquire educational, consultation, and training experiences to improve effectiveness in working with diverse populations including special needs and (b) advocate for appropriate accommodations and accessibility for students with disabilities. Throughout the *Standards*, any reference to "the individual" should be interpreted to include those students with disabilities and special needs.

The School Counselor, NCLB, and the Achievement Gap

The No Child Left Behind Act of 2001 (NCLB, 2006; see Chapter 1) is the major federal law related to education in Grades K to 12. It is based on the principles of accountability, efficacy, parental involvement, and local control/flexibility. The stated purpose of the legislation is to raise academic achievement for all students and to close the achievement gap. NCLB provides definitions of professional personnel in the schools, including the school counselor:

> The term "school counselor" means an individual who has documented competence in counseling children and adolescents in a school setting and who—
>
> (A) is licensed by the State or certified by an independent professional regulatory authority;
>
> (B) in the absence of such State licensure or certification, possesses national certification in school counseling or a specialty of counseling granted by an independent professional organization; or
>
> (C) holds a minimum of a master's degree in school counseling from a program accredited by the Council for Accreditation of Counseling and Related Educational Programs or the equivalent. (Sec. 5421[e][3]))

Today's School Counselor

"Professional school counselors: Acquire educational, consultation and training experiences to improve awareness, knowledge, skills and effectiveness in working with diverse populations: [and] advocate for appropriate accommodations and accessibility for students with disabilities" (ASCA, 2010a, E.2.c & d).

There are many inequities in our schools across ethnic and socioeconomic groups when it comes to the achievement gap for special education students. Professional school counselors need to provide responsive services and report accountability evidence for how students, including those with disabilities, are making adequate progress in closing the achievement gap.

The Role of the Professional School Counselor in Providing Special Education Services

Although ASCA recommends a counselor-to-student ratio of 1:250 (2005b), national student-to-school counselor ratios averaged 465:1 in the 2008–2009 school year (U.S. Department of Education, 2010), and many counselors either work in more than one school or are the sole counselor in their school. Counselors face myriad expectations and requests from administrators, teachers, and parents, often without clearly delineated roles and responsibilities when it comes to special education. The local education agency needs to provide everyone on the special education team with specific expectations for meeting the needs of students with disabilities. School counselors can and should be self-advocates for the ethical responsibility of serving this population through the school counseling program.

The guiding questions in the decision tree provided in Figure 2.2 can be useful for school counselors to begin the process of assessing how their school counseling program can meet the needs of every student. This tool can guide school counselors in (a) developing the **foundation** of the program by establishing both the baseline student data and team members with whom to collaborate, (b) identifying a **delivery system** that includes both counseling services and system support, (c) establishing a **management system** for the program by starting with a needs assessment, and (d) using **accountability** to demonstrate that the program is making a difference for students.

School Counselors and Advocacy

The increasing diversity in our schools has brought many challenges for all educators, including school counselors. There is a variety of socioeconomic characteristics that can impact students, such as poverty, unemployment, and homelessness. Students and families from ethnic minority groups should not be disadvantaged because of language difficulties, lack of access to preschool programs, or cultural differences (Santos de Barona & Barona, 2006). Given that 90% of public school teachers are of European American descent and that over 42% of students attending public schools are considered to be an ethnic or racial minority, many school personnel may be unaware or lack adequate understanding of the unique characteristics and experiences of their students

Figure 2.2 Guiding Questions for the School Counselor

Do I have a school counseling program mission statement for the purpose and focus of services to address the academic, personal/social, and career needs of each and every student, which includes students with disabilities?

Create a mission statement of no more than 3-4 sentences that clearly links the school counseling program to the educational process of each and every student.

Use your mission statement to guide the school counseling program: share with members of your school community (i.e., students, teachers, administrators, parents).

Have I disaggregated the data for my case load that includes data on students with disabilities?

Access data for my school and disaggregate for my caseload.

Baseline data established.

Have I contacted members of the special education team?

Talk with my principal and members of the special education team.

List of names and titles for special education team. Contact each individual for an introduction.

Have I completed a needs assessment to determine services and resources for all students, which includes students with disabilities?

Complete needs assessment. Collect information from students, teachers, support personnel, and parents. Use a variety of methods (e.g., online survey, paper and pencil) to collect the information.

School counseling program addresses needs of students with disabilities.

Have I identified a school counseling curriculum to meet the academic, personal/social, and career development needs of the student population I am serving?

Crosswalk guidance lessons, individual and small group planning, and responsive services to National Standards by grade level, developmental needs, and special populations.

School counseling program addresses needs of students with disabilities.

Is it clear that the services provided to students have a positive effect?

Accountability system developed and initiated. Collect and analyze data.

Accountability system is used to report results of school counseling program services meeting needs of students with disabilities.

and may incorrectly interpret children's behaviors and approaches to learning (Santos de Barona & Barona, 2006). Unfortunately, many teachers view differences in learning as deficiencies because they have not been adequately trained in issues of cultural diversity. This situation can result in students feeling disenfranchised resulting in poor school attendance, low achievement, and behavioral difficulties (Santos de Barona & Barona, 2006).

There is a disproportionate representation of culturally and linguistically diverse students in special education programs nationwide. *Disproportionality* is defined as an overrepresentation or underrepresentation of a particular group in special or gifted education programs, respectively, related to the overall student population. Research has shown that "a child's race and ethnicity are significantly related to the probability that he or she will be inappropriately identified as disabled" (National Education Association, NEA, 2007, p. 6). Zhang and Katsiyannis (2002) found support for concerns regarding overrepresentation of African American and American Indian/Alaska Native students in all disability categories (i.e., emotional behavioral disorders, learning disabilities, intellectual disabilities); Hispanic and Asian/Pacific Islander students were found to be underrepresented in all categories (see Table 2.1). According to the NEA (2007), disproportionality is a concern because

- Once a student is receiving special education services, he or she tends to remain in special education classes.

- The student is more likely to have access to a less rigorous curriculum.

- Expectations for the student may be lower, which can lead to fewer academic and postsecondary opportunities.

- Students in special education programs may have less access to their academically able peers.

- The student may be socially stigmatized.

- It can significantly contribute to racial separation.

Therefore, there is a need for continuous monitoring of school and environmental factors that may adversely affect the ability for all students to succeed. School counselors can provide the advocacy leadership so that discriminatory practices do not marginalize particular student groups (see Table 2.2).

Table 2.1   Child Count IDEA, Part B, by Disability (50 States and Washington, DC)

Race/Ethnicity	Total public school student population by race/ethnicity (*N* = 49,293,000)	Students 3- to 21-year olds served under IDEA by race/ethnicity (*N* = 6,606,000)	All disabilities	Specific learning disability	Intellectual disabilities	Emotional disturbance
White	58%	58%	57%	53%	49%	57%
Black	16%	20%	20%	20%	31%	29%
Hispanic	20%	18%	19%	24%	17%	12%
Asian/Pacific Islander	4%	2%	2%	2%	2%	1%
American Indian/ Alaska Native	1%	2%	2%	2%	1%	2%

Source: U.S. Department of Education, Office of Special Education Programs, Individuals With Disabilities Act IDEA/Data for 2007-2008. Analytic tool used to build table retrieved from https://www.ideadata.org.

Promoting Inclusion

As discussed in Chapter 1, the concept of inclusion has grown rapidly over the past half-century, with students with disabilities moving out of segregated "special education" classrooms into general education settings. Although many students and staff now readily accept the practice, others need time and assistance in making the practice work in the classroom. This is a helpful role for the school counselor to assume. Knowledge of and agreement with the least restrictive environment for all students allows counselors to share their belief that all students benefit from the legal requirement to educate students with

Table 2.2 The School Counselor and Advocacy Leadership

Goal	Strategies
Be visible and have a voice.	Collaborate with special education teachers to provide in-house professional development. Keep teachers informed and model how to work with other professionals.
Change beliefs and attitudes of teachers and students.	Use data, role models, and students who have succeeded to highlight what is currently known about disabilities, and the price paid when some students are marginalized and not afforded the same opportunities.
Be aware of disproportionality patterns.	Explore online local school district and state department of education data, and data from school counselor records. Monitor current enrollments as well as enrollments over time and disaggregate the data over a number of characteristics to see the "big picture."
Ensure access to guidance and counseling activities for all students.	As part of the management system for the school counseling program, use data to monitor services provided and who participates, and determine amount of time being spent on responsive services. Develop action plans so that students with disabilities have access to and are taking advantage of services provided through the school counseling program.
Address issues at both the systemic and individual levels.	Be involved in school committees that deal with policies and procedures. Identify ways that the school counseling program contributes to the academic success of students with disabilities. Become a collaborator with special education teachers and tap into their expertise to identify ways to support students with disabilities.
Actively engage in developing a positive school culture.	Be the "heart of the school" and counter negative and exclusionary practices. Focus on positive reinforcement with administrators, teachers, students, and parents to build a caring positive school culture.

disabilities with their peers to the maximum extent possible. School counselors can work with students to inculcate the social skills and beliefs that support equity for all students. Promoting acceptance of all students, including those with disabilities, is a primary task of the school counselor and can be completed through modeling, teaching, and promoting inclusive practices. "Because the ultimate success or failure of inclusion will depend on the commitment and willingness of all to put it into practice, [the participation of school counselors] is absolutely critical" (Greer, Greer, & Woody, 1995, ¶27).

Advocacy for Parents, Students, and Staff

School counselors, in consultation with special educators, disseminate information about disabilities to families who may have entered the world of special education for the first time. Consultation and advocacy with parents takes place before, during, and after the special education eligibility process (see Chapter 3 for a discussion of the school counselor's role in the process of identifying students for eligibility for special education services).

School counselors are often the point of contact for students and families. When there is a behavior or academic difficulty, parents and students often turn to the counselor for advice and support. Generally, parents will communicate with the school counselor because they see the counselor as the person most familiar with the student and the student's needs (Greer et al., 1995). The school counselor's role ranges from suggesting interventions to the parents and staff, to helping general education teachers develop behavior improvement plans, to referring families to outside counseling.

When first learning about potential behavioral, learning, or developmental disabilities, parents often have many questions about the special education process and about specific disabilities. It is important for the school counselor to develop a facilitative relationship with the family and to keep the channels of communication open (Bowen & Glenn, 1998). This allows parents to talk about their fears and concerns, while explaining the process, step by step. During the multidisciplinary meeting, the school counselor, along with other professional team members, advocates for the best interests of the student and provide support to parents during any team meetings, which can be daunting to even the savviest of parents. During the evaluation process, which by law can take up to 60 days (depending on state guidelines), continue to support the student, parents, and teachers.

The advocacy role does not cease when the eligibility door opens. When students are identified as eligible for special education, parents have an overwhelming need for information.

Parents develop wishes, expectations, and dreams for their children, even before the child is born. At a minimum, parents wish for a healthy baby ("We don't care whether it's a boy or a girl, just as long as it's healthy" is the cliché that is repeated over and over), and they assume that it will be so. The discovery that the wished-for child has a disability can be seen as destroying the hopes and dreams held by the parents. (Taub, 2006, ¶5)

Some parents may experience sadness that their child has a disability and grieve for the loss of the "dream child." Others may be relieved that their concerns about their child have been answered, and still others may require information about a particular disability, the impact of a label on the student and siblings, or the nature of the services. "Parents need knowledge about the nature, etiology and general prognosis of the disabling condition and education in parenting. They need a supportive and constructive environment in which to express their feelings" (Bowen & Glenn, 1998, ¶24). Special education personnel can answer these questions and concerns as well; however, when the school counselor has been with the family since the beginning of the process, parents and students may continue to turn to them for understanding and support.

Summary

The ASCA National Model (2005a) provides school counselors with the framework to organize and deliver a comprehensive developmentally appropriate program focusing on the identified needs and demonstrated effectiveness of a variety of counseling services. The professional school counselor as a student advocate is aware of the legal and ethical guidelines in providing support to students with disabilities. Further, understanding and addressing disproportionality will assure that each and every student has the opportunity to succeed. The school counselor's leadership role in advocacy includes students, parents, and staff. Providing information, offering support, and identifying resources can be best accomplished through collaboration and teaming. This process of collaboration and teaming to meet the needs of students with disabilities and their parents is further discussed in Chapter 3, which provides guidance on how to build effective teams using a collaborative consultation model. Procedures are clarified through the use of related forms and templates that are included in the chapter.

Reflective Questions

- How do I ensure that the needs of special education students are met through the school counseling program?

- What role do I play when it comes to collaboration and teaming?

Collaboration and Teaming

Meet the Needs of Students With Disabilities

Special Education Services

The School Counseling Program

- Evaluation and identification of students requiring special education services

- Development of academic strategies, interventions, and education programs to support students with disabilities

- Collaborative consultation
- Advocacy
- Inclusion
- Transitions
- Accountability

- Understanding and participating on school multidisciplinary and special education teams

- Collaboration with general education and special education staff

A Shared Vision of Special Education and School Counseling

Have you ever been part of a team? Maybe a debate team or athletic team or quiz bowl team? Maybe work on teams as part of your responsibilities as a professional school counselor? Teams work best (i.e., are effective) when each member brings a unique contribution, collaborates with other team members, and works toward common goals. Teams allow school counselors to be more efficient in the services they provide through the school counseling program. With the average national caseload for school counselors at 465:1 (ASCA, 2010C; U.S. Department of Education, 2010), school counselors must develop collaborations and partnerships to be sure that every student experiences success through access to rigorous courses, a quality curriculum, and the necessary educational support (House & Hayes, 2002). Effective collaborative teams can help school counselors be more efficient in the services they provide through the school counseling program.

Collaboration and teaming is one of the themes in the ASCA National Model for School Counseling Programs (2005a). Because of their unique skills and training, professional school counselors are distinctly qualified in helping to "build effective teams by encouraging genuine collaboration among all school staff to work toward the common goals of equity, access and academic success for every student" (ASCA, 2005a, p. 25). It is essential that the school counselor be viewed as an important contributing member of the school staff and relevant to the school mission. In order to make a contribution and be relevant, school counselors need to

- team and consult with teachers to improve student achievement,

- provide consultation for teachers on children's developmental needs,

- create mentoring and peer counseling programs to provide support for all students,

- assess barriers to student learning,

- collect and interpret student data for use in helping educators engage in needed reforms,

- advocate for rigorous academic preparation and experiences to broaden all students' educational and career options, and

- link with community agencies to provide the widest range of resources for students and their families (Musheno & Talbert, 2002).

The skills counselors need to be effective include collaboration and teaming, leadership, assessment and use of data to bring about change, advocacy, and counseling and coordination. These are the five skills that will equip "transformed" school counselors to become leaders in educational reform and to advocate for improving all students' academic success (The Education Trust, 1997)—and this goal of academic success applies to students receiving special education services.

Building Effective Teams

School counselors have access to a body of literature on how to build effective teams and can draw on their training in communication, decision making, group process, consultation, human behavior, change process, personality, human development, and assessment. School counselors understand that communication, shared aims, and decision making are key issues for teams (Larkin & Callaghan, 2005). School counselors understand group process through one or more models, such as forming, storming, norming, and performing (Tuckman, 1965) or as initial, transition, working, and final stages (Corey & Corey, 2002). School counselors know how to differentiate between a "loose group" and an "effective team": A *loose group* is a number of individuals brought together to achieve a task; an *effective team* is defined as a supportive social structure with each individual adapting one's behavior to optimize a personal contribution to the team (Sheard & Kakabadse, 2002). Key factors that collectively differentiate a loose group from an effective team include (Sheard & Kakabadse, 2002):

1. Goals that are clearly defined and understood by all.

2. Priorities that provide cohesive team alignment.

3. Roles and responsibilities that are agreed on and clearly understood by individuals on the team.

4. Self-awareness of appropriate behavior that meets team needs.

5. Leadership that is catalytic.

6. Group dynamics as a social system, which are established and accepted.

7. Communication that is open dialogue.

Figure 3.1 Effective Teams: The Ecological Perspective

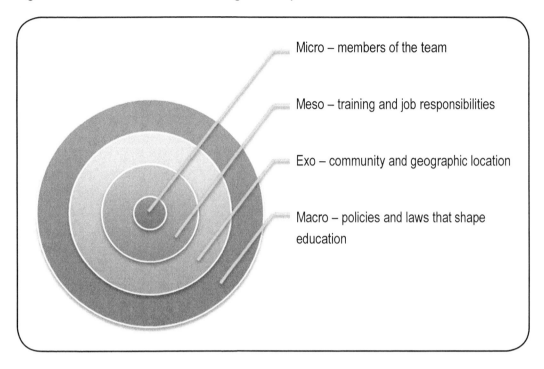

Micro – members of the team

Meso – training and job responsibilities

Exo – community and geographic location

Macro – policies and laws that shape education

8. Context that is influenced, but not controlled, by the organization (i.e., school).

9. Infrastructure that provides stable support from the organization (i.e., school).

From an ecological perspective, effective teams are social systems comprising micro, meso, exo, and macro components that interact to form a supportive social structure (Figure 3.1). The *micro* component is represented by the individual members of the team. *Meso* components are the "linking" components between individual team members and the school environment, such as training and job responsibilities. The *exo* is the context in which the school is situated, such as the community and geographic location. The *macro* component comprises the policies and laws that shape the educational enterprise. Some models also include a *chrono* component to capture the patterns of events and transitions over time.

Interprofessional working teams are not a new concept and are widespread across a variety of work settings (e.g., school teams, health care teams, community mental health teams). With increasing costs and decreasing human resources in our schools, there is a need to tap into effective teams to achieve

Multidisciplinary School-Based Teams

Crisis – Crisis Team

CST – Child Study Team

MDT- Multidisciplinary Team

PST – Problem Solving Team

RTI – Response to Intervention Team

SAT – Student Assistance Team

SBT – School-Based Team

SIT – Student Intervention Team

SPMT – Student Progress Monitoring Team

SSI – Student Support & Intervention

SST – Student Support Team

SWAT – Schoolwide Assistance Team

TAT – Teacher Assistance Team

quality and efficient services in support of academic success for all students, which includes students receiving special education services.

Teams are a small number of members with the appropriate mix of expertise, committed to a meaningful purpose with achievable performance goals, and held collectively responsible to complete a specific task (Michan & Rodger, 2005). To be effective, external structures and individual team members need to be aligned with agreed objectives and monitoring systems, shared responsibilities, defined roles and boundaries, pooled resources, and opportunities to make a contribution. Each professional as a member of the team plays a unique role; every member of the team needs to understand and appreciate the role of others on the team (Larkin & Callaghan, 2005). Clarification of roles from the onset will help to alleviate problems and negative consequences that impede effective teams.

Effective Interprofessional Collaboration: A Teaming Approach

Using an interprofessional collaboration and teaming approach is one of the best ways to build an effective team to meet the needs of students receiving special education services. Over 50 years ago, Bradley (1956) advocated for an interdisciplinary teamwork approach in special education by considering "the advantages of marshalling, for the ultimate benefit of children, the wisdom and skills of a variety of specialists" (p. 5). The Individuals With Disabilities Education Act (IDEA, 2006) specifies that individual education program (IEP) decisions be made by a team (Sec. 614[d][1][b]). It is essential, in this time of inadequate funding and increasing needs of school-aged children and adolescents, that professionals collaborate and team on issues of policy and practice to maximize their contributions to elementary and secondary education (Romano & Kachgal, 2004).

Collaboration and teaming means building a team from individuals that work together and share responsibility for results (Anderson-Butcher & Ashton, 2004). This definition implies that no single professional alone can address the needs of a given student receiving special education services. Research has shown that effective teams have (a) well-defined and forward-looking purpose that is relevant, (b) goals that link purpose with outcomes, (c) team leadership with team members agreeing and sharing leadership functions, (d) regular patterns of communication to share ideas and information, (e) cohesion as a sense of camaraderie and involvement generated by working together over time, and (f) high levels of mutual respect (Michan & Rodger, 2005).

Collaborative consultation is a process combining direct and indirect approaches so that the school counselor can be an advocate for special education students. As school-based consultants, school counselors work with teachers, parents, and others in the community in developing a school culture that understands and embraces students with disabilities as important members of the school. As consultants, school counselors need to understand the process and outcomes of effective collaborative consultation across both multidisciplinary school-based teams and special education teams.

One of the primary tenets of special education law is that no single individual, except perhaps the parent or guardian, makes a singular decision for a student with disabilities. From the time a student is referred for assessment for special education eligibility, the approach is that of collaboration and teaming. "In collaboration, no one person is considered to be the expert; the expectation is that everyone has expertise to contribute and that individuals can learn from each other" (Paulsen, 2010, p. 89). Counselors participate in a broad spectrum of interprofessional teams that generally fall into two categories, multidisciplinary school-based teams and special education teams. A school counselor's ability to use their consultative skills as part of an interpersonal and interdisciplinary approach to special education is a critical part of successful planning for student outcomes.

Multidisciplinary School-Based Teams

Perhaps one of the most important teaming roles for school counselors is participating in multidisciplinary team meetings. Multidisciplinary school-based teams have many names, such as student intervention team (SIT), student assistance team (SAT), teacher assistance team (TAT), student support and intervention (SSI), or response to intervention (RTI) team, but the name itself does not matter: These teams are formed for the sole purpose of bringing together a body of professionals who meet to discuss the needs of and brainstorm ideas to assist a student. School counselors are members of these teams

Figure 3.2 The Role of the School Counselor Before, During, and After Special Education Evaluation and Eligibility Decisions

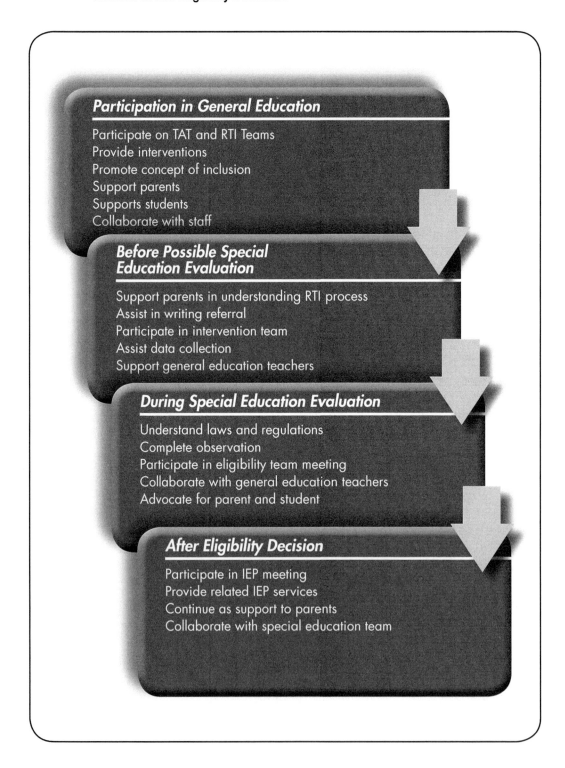

Participation in General Education

Participate on TAT and RTI Teams
Provide interventions
Promote concept of inclusion
Support parents
Supports students
Collaborate with staff

Before Possible Special Education Evaluation

Support parents in understanding RTI process
Assist in writing referral
Participate in intervention team
Assist data collection
Support general education teachers

During Special Education Evaluation

Understand laws and regulations
Complete observation
Participate in eligibility team meeting
Collaborate with general education teachers
Advocate for parent and student

After Eligibility Decision

Participate in IEP meeting
Provide related IEP services
Continue as support to parents
Collaborate with special education team

and may assume the role of the team leader. Students experiencing difficulty in or outside of school that impacts school performance are discussed during multidisciplinary team meetings. Teams are usually composed of the school psychologist, school social worker, school counselor, general education teacher, special education teacher, administrator or designee, and other professionals who are integral to the issues affecting the student.

The multidisciplinary school-based team designates the committee members and the focus of the team. Team members document their (a) involvement, (b) suggested and applied strategies, (c) professional responsibilities, and (d) meeting dates to assess the impact of the interventions. These teams operate in both general education and special education spheres and are part of the school's universal screening procedures (see Figure 3.2). Operating in a collaborative and collegial manner that focuses on teamwork helps achieve positive student benefits. "Thoughtful reflection and productive collaborations with individuals in the school building (e.g., counselors, behavioral specialists, special educators) allow teachers to become engaged in this diagnostic process rather than reluctant to work with a particular child and/or resistant to the possibility of change" (Regan, 2009, p. 62).

The responsibility of the school counselor may be "to the team . . . directly to the child . . . or indirectly to the child, supporting him or her through others on the team" (Rock & Leff, 2007, p. 319). The role of the counselor is never static and changes according to the needs of the team and the student.

Teacher Assistance Teams (TAT)

If a classroom teacher experiences difficulty with a particular student, or has questions about the student's academic or behavioral issues, TAT provides an informal process for consulting with specialists in the building. TATs are "committees of general education teachers and other education specialists whose goal is to effectively design and implement academic and behavior interventions to meet the needs of difficult to teach students" (Baumberger & Harper, 2007, p. 7). Generally, no notes are taken during the TAT meeting, and the goal is to brainstorm ideas the classroom teacher may not have considered. This is a low-key method of gathering advice from colleagues and does not require parental permission (although teacher concerns may be shared with the parents) or administrative involvement. In a nonthreatening team meeting, the school counselor is an objective colleague who can help facilitate the meeting and can offer new suggestions for the classroom teacher to implement.

Crisis Teams

Crisis teams are often composed of the same committee members as other multidisciplinary school-based teams, but the work of this team is to intervene in a crisis situation, such as dealing with the death of a student or faculty member, community issues (assaults), random acts of violence (school shootings), terrorism (9/11), issues relating to the Internet (cyberbullying), police activity (drugs), and mental health issues (suicide). Crisis teams are formed (a) to assist in defusing the impact of crisis situations by supporting the students and staff or (b) to prevent a crisis from occurring.

RTI Teams

The concept of RTI began as a medical model that relied on established benchmarks and continuous data monitoring to drive decisions, with increasing intensity in treatment (Novosel & Deshler, 2010). As discussed in Chapter 1, RTI's emergence in the education field offered an alternative approach to the IQ discrepancy model for identifying students with learning disabilities. In the school setting, RTI is a multitier approach that incorporates both general and special education systems and is an example of what IDEA refers to as a scientifically or research-based practice (IDEA Regulations, 34 CFR 300.306–309, 2006), focusing on prevention, assessment, and accountability (Paulson, 2010, p. 4)

The RTI school-based team monitors academic progress for the student body as a whole (Tier 1), small numbers of children (Tier 2), or individual interventions or referral for services (Tier 3). Interventions under RTI can be academic and instructional (with input from teachers or instructional specialists), or behavioral (with involvement from school counselors, teachers, behavior specialists, and other educators). Each school or district has its own RTI process that identifies students requiring interventions and the specific nature of those interventions. Generally, however, it is the classroom teacher who identifies a struggling student and seeks assistance from the RTI team; this may be an informal or formal process

The Role of the School Counselor in the RTI Framework

As more school divisions embrace the RTI model, the role of the school counselor increases in responsibility. The school counselor participates in a school's approach to RTI (see Figure 3.3) in a variety of ways:

- Leading the RTI team: Because school counselors have collaborative consultation team building and team management skills, they might lead the prereferral intervention, calling the members together, taking notes, and following through on the decision-making process.

- Participating as a team member: As progress monitoring occurs, the RTI team uses the data to monitor individual student progress and to evaluate instructional approaches.

- Assessing the data: The school counselor, along with other team members, assumes accountability for student progress and makes suggestions for further interventions, including a possible referral for a special education evaluation.

- Implementing an intervention: In any RTI tier, students with behavioral issues may be referred to the school counselor for an intervention, such as a social skills group, short-term counseling, or individual "check-in time" with a student.

- Promoting a schoolwide approach: Supporting the mission of RTI.

- Assisting the team in moving forward: The school counselor can provide knowledge of the special education process and when prereferral interventions need to become a special education evaluation.

- Advocating for the parents: Parents may be confused by the RTI approach and benefit from the counselor's ability to explain the process and interventions.

Figure 3.3   The Role of the School Counselor in RTI

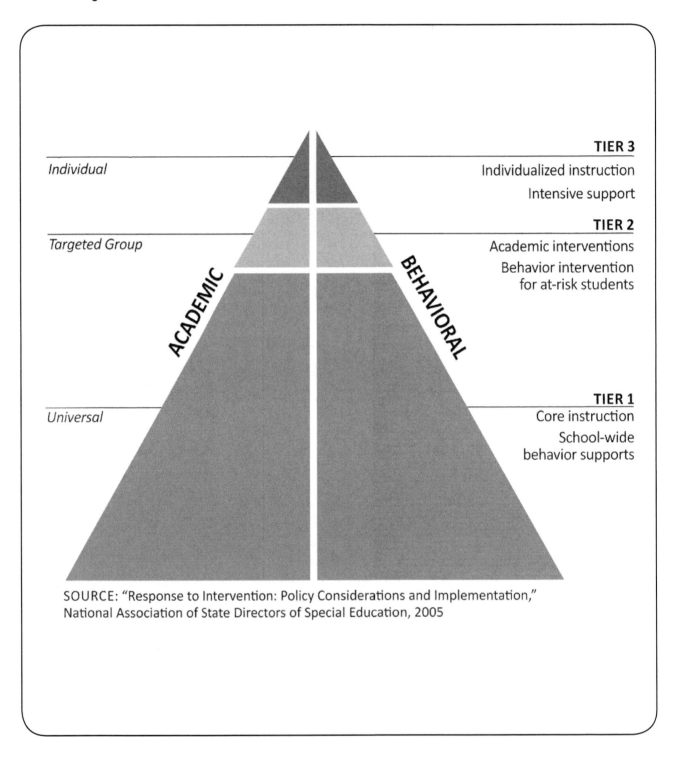

Individual

Targeted Group

Universal

ACADEMIC

BEHAVIORAL

TIER 3
Individualized instruction
Intensive support

TIER 2
Academic interventions
Behavior intervention
for at-risk students

TIER 1
Core instruction
School-wide
behavior supports

SOURCE: "Response to Intervention: Policy Considerations and Implementation,"
National Association of State Directors of Special Education, 2005

(see Request for Intervention Team Review Form, end of this chapter). The RTI team reviews information on the student to identify the specific area of need, whether academic or social/emotional and behavioral, and develops an action plan to respond to the student's need (see Intervention Team Problem-Solving Meeting Form, end of this chapter). The planned research-based intervention is monitored and evaluated for effectiveness.

The RTI model is built on the concept of a team that monitors student progress through ongoing assessment. Schoolwide practices enable continuous monitoring of students who are struggling either academically or behaviorally, through a tiered approach to interventions that become increasingly more intense. Special education evaluation and eligibility is usually considered as a Tier 3 intervention. RTI can be useful in the special education eligibility process (Virginia Department of Education, 2009) by:

- Helping the eligibility team decide if more evaluation data are needed.

- Documenting that the student received high quality research-based instruction in general education settings delivered by qualified personnel.

- Providing data to the eligibility team as one part of the evaluation process to determine if the student has a disability requiring special education and related services.

Special Education Teams

Child Find Team

Child Find is required by IDEA (34 C.F.R. Part 300); it is a screening process that seeks out and identifies children with disabilities or children at risk and refers them for appropriate services. This process includes preschool age children who exhibit delays and private school

---

Special Education Teams

Child Find Team

Special Education Referral Team

Special Education Eligibility Team

IEP (Individualized Education Program) Team

MDR (Manifest Determination Review) Team

children. The team may be composed of an administrator (or designee), special and general education teachers, school psychologist, school social worker, school counselor, the parents and/or guardians, and other school specialists as needed, such as a speech and language clinician, school nurse, and reading teacher. Data to be analyzed may include past report cards, standardized group assessments, permanent records, observations, and parental input. The Child Find Team can decide to refer the student for special education evaluation.

Special Education Referral Team

Although the name of the team and its composition depends on state and local departments of education (i.e., SEA and LEA) directives, the purpose of the special education referral team is to monitor prereferral interventions in the general education classroom. Even after interventions, some students may still exhibit a lack of academic progress or behaviors that are of concern to school staff and parents or guardians. In many instances the school counselor has already been involved with the student, the parents, and teachers during the process of implementing interventions, especially if behavior issues are of concern. It may have been the school counselor who contacted the parent about behavior or emotional issues in the first place; in the case of secondary students, the counselor often has established a relationship with the student and family built on scheduling classes, collecting and using classroom and individual student data, and making recommendations for the future.

The school-based referral process (see Figure 3.4) is vital in the application of best practices: often the recommendations put forward by the intervention team (and perhaps monitored by the counselor) make a difference in whether or not the student will be evaluated for special education. The collaborative process of listening, strategizing, formulating goals, and communicating in a respectful manner produces ideas that benefit the student, family, and school. Material discussed and analyzed includes grades, attendance, standardized test results, behavior, medical issues, private evaluations, and teacher and parent input.

Referral for Special Education Evaluation. After assessing the data and determining that the student is still not making sufficient progress, the student's parents, the classroom teacher, administrator, or other concerned adult completes a referral for a special education evaluation to determine eligibility for special education. After receiving an evaluation referral, the team has 10 business days to convene the school-based evaluation committee. If the committee decides to refer the student for an evaluation, they obtain written permission from the parents/guardians and the evaluation process starts;

Figure 3.4 The School-Based Special Education Referral Process

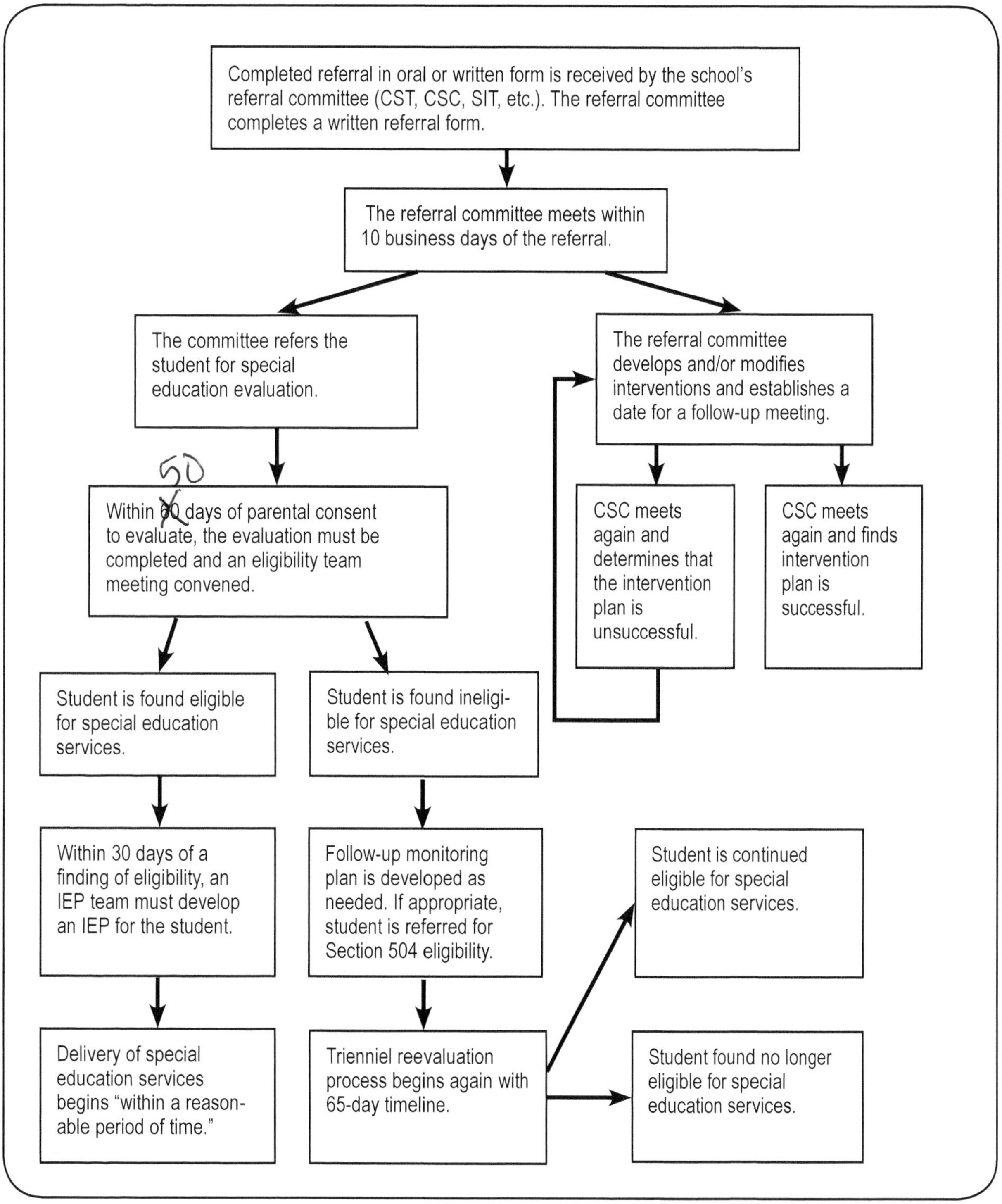
Completed referral in oral or written form is received by the school's referral committee (CST, CSC, SIT, etc.). The referral committee completes a written referral form.
The referral committee meets within 10 business days of the referral.
The committee refers the student for special education evaluation.
The referral committee develops and/or modifies interventions and establishes a date for a follow-up meeting.
Within 60 days of parental consent to evaluate, the evaluation must be completed and an eligibility team meeting convened.
CSC meets again and determines that the intervention plan is unsuccessful.
CSC meets again and finds intervention plan is successful.
Student is found eligible for special education services.
Student is found ineligible for special education services.
Within 30 days of a finding of eligibility, an IEP team must develop an IEP for the student.
Follow-up monitoring plan is developed as needed. If appropriate, student is referred for Section 504 eligibility.
Student is continued eligible for special education services.
Delivery of special education services begins "within a reasonable period of time."
Trienniel reevaluation process begins again with 65-day timeline.
Student found no longer eligible for special education services.

Note. Regulatory guidance for IDEA timelines is located at 34 C.F.R. Parts 300.301(c)(1), 300.323(c)(1), and 300.343. Timeframes established by states take precedence over timelines required by IDEA.

federal guidelines state that the initial evaluation must be completed within a 60-day time period. (The committee might decide not to pursue an evaluation, and instead write an intervention plan suggesting continuing strategies for progress and improvement and providing a timeline for continuous monitoring of the student.)

Writing a Special Education Referral for an Evaluation. Often, the school counselor is asked to assist the classroom teacher or administrator in writing a referral for a special education evaluation. Because the referral will be viewed by many evaluators and the parents, it is important to follow guidelines for writing objective, but complete, referrals. Although the classroom teacher may be at a point of wanting the child "out of" the general education classroom, and "into" special education because of continuous behavior or academic issues, the referral should not reveal any hidden biases of the teacher or stereotyping of the student. The school counselor may have a more objective view of the student based on proximity and amount of time spent with the student. Each school division has paperwork for a school-based special education referral; forms and timelines are at the discretion of individual SEAs and LEAs.

Writing Teacher Narratives. The general education classroom teacher often completes a teacher narrative as one component of the evaluation. Because the documentation used in determining eligibility for special education services is considered a legal document, it is important that teachers and specialists clearly, objectively, and appropriately complete a narrative of the student's class participation, academic progress, involvement with peers and adults, and behavior difficulties. School counselors may be called upon to assist teachers in writing these narratives, which are included as part of the special education eligibility packet. In some cases, a teacher with student concerns may have waited for RTI interventions to be assessed, the special education referral process, and the 60 days (federal guidelines; individual states may vary) needed for evaluation. Such timelines may leave a teacher feeling overwhelmed, especially since the outcome of eligibility often depends on the impact of the student's educational performance in the classroom.

The school counselor can assist classroom teachers in completing the teacher narrative by providing phrases and comments that objectively describe the student and avoid inappropriate explanations or biased comments. The teacher narrative should emphasize objectivity, data, and precise detail rather than phrases that, although accurate, are not professionally appropriate. School staff should remain truthful but not write anything that could be harmful or prejudicial to the student. School counselors can remind teachers that the student's parents or guardian will be hearing information that may be difficult to

Figure 3.5 Sample Teacher Narrative Form

Student __HOSEA ROZELL__   Date __2/24/2011__

School __JEFFERSON ELEM.__   Teacher __MRS. TRURO__

Subject __MATH__   Grade __4TH__

Current Student Grades: F IN MATH 1ST AND 2ND QUARTER

Other Informal or Formal Assessment Data: HE MISSED THE MATH TEST, AND DID NOT MAKE IT UP BECAUSE HE WAS ABSENT SO MUCH.
Preferred: HOSEA HAS NOT BEEN ABLE TO COMPLETE ANY ASSESSMENT DATA BECAUSE HE HAS DIFFICULTY CONCENTRATING, OR HE WAS ABSENT.

Attendance: LATE ALL THE TIME. HE IS OUT OF SCHOOL AT LEAST TWO DAYS A WEEK. I DON'T KNOW WHAT IS WRONG WITH HIM.
Preferred: HOSEA HAS DIFFICULTY GETTING TO SCHOOL ON TIME. HE IS OFTEN ABSENT AND SOMETIMES IT IS DIFFICULT TO KNOW WHY HE DID NOT ATTEND SCHOOL.

Class participation: HE SHOUTS OUT ANSWERS THAT ARE INCORRECT. HIS PARTICIPATION IS INAPPROPRIATE SINCE HE DOESN'T KNOW THE ANSWERS.
Preferred: HOSEA APPEARS TO WANT TO PARTICIPATE IN CLASS DISCUSSIONS, BUT HE OFTEN SHOUTS OUT INCORRECT ANSWERS.

Academic Concerns: HE HAS NO STRENGTHS IN ANY ACADEMIC AREAS.
Preferred: ALTHOUGH HOSEA APPEARS TO WANT TO DO WELL, HIS ACADEMIC STRENGTH IS NOT IN MATH.

Academic Strengths: POOR PERFORMANCE IN ALL AREAS OF MATH. HE CAN'T ADD AT ALL, AND HE NEVER DOES THE WORD PROBLEMS. HE NEEDS TO REPEAT THE 6TH GRADE.
Preferred: IN MATH, HOSEA HAS DIFFICULTY WITH CALCULATIONS AND WORD PROBLEMS. HE IS ABLE TO READ THE PROBLEMS, BUT HAS NO IDEA HOW TO BEGIN TO START THE PROCESS.

Work Habits: CLASS WORK IS USUALLY INCOMPLETE SINCE HE SPENDS HIS TIME READING MANGA.
Preferred: HE HAS A HARD TIME FOCUSING ON HIS WORK, AND IS OFTEN DISTRACTED BY HIS FAVORITE READING MATERIAL (MANGA).

Peer and Adult Relationships: HE WON'T LISTEN TO ME WHEN I TELL HIM TO PUT AWAY THOSE HORRID MANGA THINGS. HIS PEERS DON'T LIKE HIM IN GROUP MATH ACTIVITIES.
Preferred: HOSEA DOES NOT CONSISTENTLY FOLLOW ADULT REQUESTS AND DIRECTIONS. HIS PEERS ARE OFTEN FRUSTRATED WITH HIS INABILITY TO COMPLETE MATH GROUP ACTIVITIES.

Intervention Strategies: I CALLED HIS MOTHER 15 TIMES.
Preferred: FREQUENT PHONE CALLS TO HIS MOTHER, ESPECIALLY ABOUT HIS TARDIES AND ABSENCES.

Table 3.1   Helpful Comments for Teacher Narratives

Don't write this...	*Instead, use these phrases...*
"He doesn't know how to study."	Requires extra time to complete tests and assignments Avoids written work Does not complete class work/homework Does not turn in assignments on time Requires prompts to start work Disorganized: loses materials, papers, etc. Requires immediate feedback Notebook disorganized Difficulty staying on task
"Misbehaves all the time."	Appears lethargic, apathetic, or withdrawn Gives up easily; does not express need for assistance Easily distracted or appears to daydream Arrives to class late Frequently absent Makes frequent visits to clinic, restroom, or counselor Seeks attention inappropriately (verbal and nonverbal) Blurts out comments and talks out in class Demonstrates extremes in behavior (from sad to happy quickly and unable to cope with feelings) Moves around room without permission Is physically aggressive towards peers
"Nobody likes her."	Difficulty making friends Tends to be a loner Bullies others Teases, is teased or is a scapegoat Socially immature Can be anxious or nervous Somewhat preoccupied with sexual issues Poor hygiene Excessive mood swings
"Adults don't like him"	Resents or disregards authority figures Disregards the feelings of others Will not seek adults in stressful times Refuses to comply with rules and directions; responds negatively to staff Teases and bullies others

Table 3.1   Helpful Comments for Teacher Narratives (cont'd.)

Don't write this...	*Instead, use these phrases...*
"She's not very smart."	Math, reading, and spelling below grade level expectations Weak fine motor skills; poor handwriting and eye/hand coordination Impaired gross motor coordination Language delays; can't find words to express ideas Difficulty sequencing information Unable to complete multiple assignments Does not process oral information Performs at a level significantly below peers/grade level Consistently requires academic support
"She's very smart."	Performs at or above grade level Possesses strong verbal skills Follows written or verbal directions Works independently Takes responsibility for own learning; a self starter Participates in group and/or class discussions appropriately
"His behavior is impeccable."	Arrives to class on time; begins work promptly Completes class work and homework Comes to class with materials Maintains organized notebook Stays on task; works conscientiously Exhibits appropriate study skills Cooperates with peers; works well in small groups Demonstrates a positive attitude Asks for help from adults in an appropriate manner Demonstrates desire to achieve; is eager to please Changes tasks easily Displays positive self-esteem Thinks before acting Demonstrates being self-motivated Resists peer pressure Resolves conflicts easily Assumes leadership role

assimilate: it is their child that is being dissected and discussed by a group of professionals. For the Teacher Narrative, using a more exact phrase that has less of a negative connotation (see Figure 3.5 and Tables 3.1 and 3.2) can be the difference between initiating antipathy between the family and school staff, and providing a positive tool for the evaluation. (A blank form is included at the end of this chapter.)

Classroom Observation Form. As the process for special education becomes formalized, the role of the school counselor is critical. As part of the evaluation process the school counselor may be asked to observe the student in the classroom (see Figure 3.2) and write a clear, concise and objective report of the student's classroom performance. It is the effect of a disability on the student's academic performance that dictates whether or not a student is found eligible for specialized instruction (see end of chapter for a blank form).

Special Education Eligibility Team

The school counselor may also be a member of the eligibility team. This requires that counselors be knowledgeable about the special education process and contribute their insight in a meaningful and collaborative manner. If a student is found eligible for special education services, the counselor may participate as a member of the IEP team that writes the plan for the student. In some instances, school counselors become part of the services for students by offering school-based short-term counseling (counseling services may also be provided by a clinical social worker or the school psychologist).

IEPs are in effect for a period of 3 years; near the end of the 3-year period, the team holds a reevaluation meeting to decide if the student needs to have a new battery of assessments or if existing data are sufficient to make an eligibility decision. Counselors can expect to be part of the reevaluation team if they have been involved with the student, have knowledge of the student, or have been asked to contribute information to the team.

IEP Team

Once a student has been found eligible for special education services, the team must write an IEP as soon as possible (20 U.S.C. § 1412[2][B], [4], [6]; 1414[a][5]). After establishing the student's present level of performance, the team establishes annual goals (and short-term objectives, if required) and required services to support the student's progress. In addition, per IDEA student IEPs must include any modification in administration of state- and districtwide assessments, how the family will be kept informed, location and duration of services, extent of participation in the general education setting, and transition services (34 CFR § 300.347). The school counselor might

Table 3.2   Writing a Referral for Special Education Evaluation

Do You Do This?

1. Use objective terms to describe her behavior?

2. Keep your feelings about Sylvie in check?

3. Use relevant assessment data?

4. Describe her interactions with peers and adults, not by what others have said?

5. View Sylvie as the whole child?

6. Summarize Sylvie's strengths?

7. Identify areas of concern that led to your referral (academic, behavioral, language, social/ emotional and health)?

Try not to say this:

Unlike most of her peers, Sylvie can't remember anything in 2nd grade. She reads like a pre-K student and can barely do math. She does not bother bringing her book bag to class. I am constantly telling her to "pay attention." Her peers don't like her since she is the last to complete her work and she holds them up from going to recess. She does not know how to play and often begins to cry.

Instead, say this:

Sylvie enjoys daily morning meetings and makes appropriate contributions. With cues in the classroom, she is able to pay attention. She has difficulty remembering basic math computation facts. Her DRA reading level is 4. She often forgets her materials at home. She seems to want to perform at the level of her peers and often asks why she can't read. She has become withdrawn since the winter break and seems anxious.

provide short-term counseling as a "related service," and input into the counseling goals and the amount of time services will be provided.

Manifest Determination Review (MDR) Team

In cases involving disciplinary infractions, the MDR team determines if the student's misconduct was caused by or had a direct or substantial relationship to the disability, or if the behavior was the direct result of the school's failure to implement the IEP (34 CFR § 300.350). A school counselor may be part of the MDR team that discusses consequences and results of the discipline infraction. This process is governed by federal and state law and, as such, requires procedures that do not vary from the required task. The school counselor does not lead the MDR team review but should be familiar and comfortable with the required process and procedures.

Summary

The school counselor assumes a variety of roles in working with students, parents, and school personnel before, during, and after the special education eligibility process. The collaborative consultation model provides a framework for the school counselor to effectively work with special education personnel and students. The school counselor is a vital team member in the process of assisting students to make academic, social, and emotional growth during their education. The advent of RTI and its relationship to special education places an emphasis on the expanded role of school counselors in providing services to all students in a variety of settings.

School counselors may provide short-term counseling and transition services specifically related to an IEP requirement. They are also involved with providing advocacy services for students found ineligible for an IEP during the special education process. These roles are discussed in greater depth in Chapter 4.

Reflective Questions

- How do I build an effective team to meet the needs of students with disabilities?

- What role do I play when it comes to collaboration and teaming?

Initial Request For Intervention Team Review Form

Student _____   Date _____

Birth Date _____   Grade _____ ID# _____

School _____   Teacher _____

Parent(s) _____   Phone # _____

Language(s) spoken at home _____

Meeting requested by _____

Problems noted in

Reading	Math	Writing	Social/Behavioral

What should the student be able to do? (Attach work samples if additional information is needed.)

How have concerns been discussed with the parent?

Who should attend the meeting?   Who will contact them?

Administrator   General Education Teacher

Parent   Teacher or Counselor

Psychologist   Special Education Teacher

Social Worker   Administrator

Speech and Language Clinician

Reading Specialist

School Counselor

Problem Solving Meeting Date _____ Time _____

Student _____   Date_____

Birth Date _____   Grade _____   ID# _____

School _____   Teacher _____

Parent(s) _____   Phone # _____

Language(s) spoken at home _____

Meeting requested by _____

Current services student is receiving:

Student assets:

Statement of Concern: What academic or behavior problems is the student experiencing?
(Describe in observable/measurable terms)

What interventions have already been tried?

What should the student be able to do?

Parent Present: Yes _____   No _____

Parent Input:

Goal Statement

By (date)_____ the student will _____

_____

Possible solutions/research-based interventions:

Action Plan

Brief description of Action Plan:

Research-based intervention/strategy	Start date	Frequency/ duration	Person(s) responsible	Progress monitoring assessment & schedule

Date of follow-up meeting to evaluate progress _____

Progress Monitoring/Evaluation

Effect of Intervention on Student Academic and Behavioral Performance:

Review of Action Plan and Further Disposition (Include data sheets):

Progress made. Continue, discontinue, or alter plan_____

Additional interventions needed _____

Refer to Child Study for assessment_____

Parent requested referral to special education_____

Signatures: Team Leader_____ Teacher_____

Parent _____ Administrator _____

Teacher Narrative Form

Student _____   Date _____

School _____   Teacher _____

Subject _____   Grade _____

Current Student Grades:

Other Informal or Formal Assessment Data:

Attendance:

Class participation:

Academic Concerns:

Academic Strengths:

Work Habits:

Peer and Adult Relationships:

Intervention Strategies:

Student Classroom Observation Form

Student: _____   Date: _____

School: _____   Grade: _____

Observer Name and Position: _____

Time of Observation   From: _____   To: _____

Class/Instruction: _____   Teacher: _____

Write a brief summary of the student' academic performance, behavior, and social interactions, during the observation time. Include activities observed.

STUDENT:	100% of time	75% of time	50% of time
Arrives to class on time			
Starts work promptly			
Is attentive			
Responds positively to peers			
Exhibits age appropriate behavior			
Follows teacher directions (oral)			
Follows teacher directions (written)			
Interacts positively with teacher			
Uses accommodations			
Completes written assignments			
Participates in class discussion			
Participates in group activity			
Stays in room and/or in seat			
Completes work on time			

Comments:

Provision of Counseling Services for Students With Disabilities

Related Services Provider

Special Education Process

Role of School Counselor

- Participation in IEP team identification of related services to include short-term counseling

- Assistance with writing goals for short-term counseling and monitoring of student progress

- Collaborative consultation
- Advocacy
- Inclusion
- Transitions
- Accountability

- Responsive services to students through individual and group counseling and small group advisement

- Responsive services to parents through consultation

A Shared Vision of Special Education and School Counseling

S chool counselors provide responsive services to students and parents, including individual planning and short-term counseling to students eligible for and receiving special education services and consultation with their parents. This role also entails consultation with teachers and other support personnel, and with outside agencies as required. School counselors also have a responsibility to students who have been found ineligible for special education support services. For both types of student, the school counselor provides *individual planning* and *responsive services* (see Figure 4.1).

Figure 4.1   ASCA National Model for School Counseling Programs

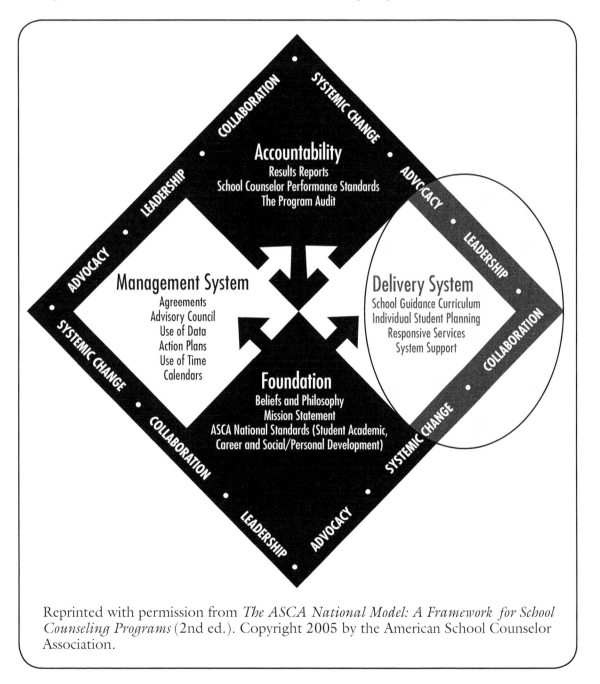

Reprinted with permission from *The ASCA National Model: A Framework for School Counseling Programs* (2nd ed.). Copyright 2005 by the American School Counselor Association.

Counseling Program Services for Students with Disabilities

Individuals With Disabilities Education Act (IDEA regulations, 2006) specify that related services offered to students with disabilities may include counseling services "provided by qualified social workers, psychologists, guidance counselors, or other qualified personnel" (34 CFR § 300.34[c][2]). The school counselor's support services for students with disabilities—in particular individual and group counseling—is part of the Delivery System element of the American School Counselor Association (ASCA) National Model (2005a). *Individual student planning* for students with individualized education programs (IEPs) focuses on helping students set personal and future goals (see Table 4.1). School counselors can support students in planning, monitoring, and managing their learning; this is particularly important for adolescents and essential for students with learning or developmental difficulties. These services can be offered one-on-one or in small groups, sometimes also involving parents and teachers. Individual student planning should help students understand and assess their interests, abilities, and skills along with monitoring strengths and challenges that are important in determining personal, educational, and occupational goals. (See Chapter 6 for a discussion on supporting students with IEPs by providing transition services and information on postsecondary opportunities.)

Table 4.1   Individual Student Planning and Responsive Services for Students With Disabilities

Individual student planning	Responsive services (via individual and group counseling)
Setting personal and future goals Postsecondary planning Assessing strengths, interests, skills, and abilities Monitoring strengths and challenges	For students: Relationships Personal concerns Developmental tasks
	In consultation with parents: Understanding school services Understanding disabilities Supporting behavior plans Developmental considerations

The school counselor also provides *responsive services* through short-term individual and group counseling addressing immediate needs pertaining to relationships, personal concerns, and other developmental tasks. Counselors select a theoretical framework that "meets students where they are" rather than one based on a predetermined grade level or chronological age (see Table 4.2).

Table 4.2   Counseling Strategies and Theoretical Frameworks

Approach	Focus
Adlerian	Social interest, goals of misbehavior, lifestyle assessment
Reality	Choices, consequences, wants-doing-evaluate-plan (WDEP)
Solution-focused	Solutions, not problems; scaling, what works, positive reframes, strengths
Rational emotive behavior	Thoughts/cognitions, feelings/emotions, behaviors; ABCDE model; irrational thoughts; changing beliefs to change behaviors
Cognitive behavioral	Self-talk, behavior management, reinforcement, contracts

Individual counseling is usually brief and short-term. Group counseling can be topic-specific with heterogeneous or homogeneous groups of students. Students with disabilities benefit from both types of group counseling: in homogeneous groups with peers who are dealing with similar special education needs and in heterogeneous groups where everyone can benefit from understanding and accommodating individual differences. The goal of these responsive services is to assist the student in being receptive to instruction and in successfully engaging in the learning process.

Providing Counseling as a Related Service Through the IEP

Counseling as a part of school-based interventions for students with disabilities is generally a cognitive-behavioral approach with a focus on thoughts, perceptions, and emotions that underlie or mediate the occurrence of maladaptive behaviors. The purpose of counseling is to change the overt behavior and is addressed through objectives that focus on identifying and changing thoughts to effect change in behavior. Counselors may use a variety of techniques, such as cognitive restructuring, rational-emotive behavior, problem

Appropriate Short-Term IEP Counseling Goals

Increase attendance

Comply with school/ classroom guidelines

Interact appropriately with peers and/or adults

Identify motivation behind behavior

Improve academic performance

Demonstrate attention to tasks and task effort

Exhibit appropriate verbal behavior

Manage anger

Address errors in thinking

Behave in socially appropriate ways

solving, coping skills, choices and consequences, and being solution-focused. *Counseling* should not be confused with *behavior management*, which generally is focused on increasing or decreasing target behaviors and may not address changes in thoughts, perceptions, and emotions. Clearly, IEP counseling goals and behavior improvement goals will work hand-in-hand for the best possible outcomes for the student.

It is important that the goal and objectives for counseling are clearly described and are distinguished from any behavior intervention plan in the student's IEP. Counseling *goals* should reflect anticipated results for the student; counseling *objectives* should be described in terms of changing the cognitive/emotional mediators that are presumed to underlie the target behaviors, and will lead to goal attainment. Target behaviors are stated as those that are to be increased or decreased in frequency, duration, form, and/or intensity. It is important that the objectives are written as expected outcomes that are behaviorally stated and described in measurable terms so that progress can be monitored. Data on progress should be collected and reported at least once each marking period.

The school, or school counselor, needs to collect documented evidence that clearly indicates the student will benefit from the related service of short-term counseling. This evidence can be in the form of functional behavioral assessments, behavior checklists completed by teachers and parents, discipline history, or psychological evaluations. Based on this evidence, short-term counseling can be recommended as a related service and part of the IEP team process (see Table 4.3).

Writing annual goals for counseling and monitoring progress provides the IEP team with data that demonstrate the school counselor's service delivery for the student (see Figure 4.3 for samples). Data should demonstrate how students are achieving their annual goals.

Table 4.3   Collecting Data on Current Level of Performance and Progress Monitoring

Do You Do This?

1. Look beyond the obvious?

2 Avoid drawing conclusions (i.e., "all of the time," "not going to graduate")?

3. Use concrete terms to identfy observations about in class behavior?

4. Focus on both strengths (e.g., classes attended) as well as weaknesses (e.g., classes missed)?

5. Obtain teacher descriptions of expectations?

6. Collect baseline data and monitor student progress?

Try not to say this:

> Juan seems to be spending a lot of time in the principal's office. I don't think he is able to stay in class. At this pace, he is not going to graduate.

Instead, say this:

> I noted that Juan was in the principal's office during three class periods this morning during math, English, and general science classes. Each of those teachers indicated he was not on task during study time and interfered with other students' study time. However, I noted that Juan was able to complete each of his class sessions in the afternoon for physical education, geography, and history. Each of those teachers indicates Juan does better when he knows what he needs to complete in a specified time in class.

Figure 4.3 Writing Annual Goals for Counseling and Monitoring Progress

Utilizing weekly counseling sessions of 30 minutes in a group that does not exceed five students, the student will achieve the following objective and outcomes:

Objective: By _____ (target date), the student will be able to appropriately address frustrations that take him/her off task in math as demonstrated by increased on-task behavior and work completion 90% of the time as measured by checklists and teacher observations.

Measurable Outcomes

- By _____ (target date), the student will complete 80% of all assigned work in math.

- By _____ (target date), the student will complete 85% of all assigned work in math.

- By _____ (target date), the student will complete 90% of all assigned work in math.

Strategies

Using a rational-emotive behavior approach in group counseling, the student will learn to:

- Identify frustrating situations (antecedents) that lead to off-task behavior(s).

- Describe what is frustrating (consequences) in each of these situations.

- Identify more appropriate ways to address these frustrations (disputing).

- Role-play, practice, and implement one or more of these ways to address frustrations.

Objective: By _____ (target date), the student will decrease attention-seeking misbehavior(s) in Language Arts from 6 times an hour to no more than 10 times weekly as measured by a student-rated checklist.

Measurable Outcomes

- By _____ (target date), the student will decrease attention-seeking misbehavior(s) to no more than 4 times an hour.

- By _____ (target date), the student will decrease attention-seeking misbehavior(s) to no more than 2 times an hour.

- By _____ (target date), the student will decrease attention-seeking misbehavior(s) to no more than 20 times weekly.

- By _____ (target date), the student will decrease attention-seeking misbehavior(s) to no more than 10 times weekly

Strategies

Using a solution-focused approach in group counseling, the student will learn to:

- Identify at least 10 personal strengths.

- Determine how each strength is used and receives positive attention.

- Rank on a scale of 1 to 10 the personal strengths, with 10 being what the student deems his/her best strength.

- Describe how the best personal strength can be used in each school activity during one day.

- Practice using the best personal strength throughout one school day and record positive attention that is received.

- Reflect on feelings associated with positive attention.

Students Found Ineligible for Special Education

Some students go through the eligibility process and are not found eligible for special education services. In these cases, the school might offer parents an informal but meaningful general education plan as a way of assisting the student. A team of general education teachers and specialists meets with the parents to identify appropriate strategies. Although this type of plan may not carry the legal weight of an IEP (i.e., does not fall under IDEA), the collaborative consultation team approach (see Chapter 3) again works to benefit the student. The process still includes devising strategies, delineating implementation methods, and monitoring progress. Students found ineligible for special education services can always be referred again in the future by the parents or teachers; referrals for eligibility can occur at any time during the student's school career.

School counselors play a role as part of the team in devising appropriate strategies for these students. *Responsive services* through the school counseling program include small-group advisement and individual and group counseling for students; and consultation for parents, teachers, other support personnel, and outside agencies. Small-group advisement is important to be sure every student has the goal of graduating from high school and having a postsecondary plan. *Advisement* includes counselor activities such as reviewing test scores, promotion and retention information, career decision making, course selection, test-taking strategies, and review of behavior plans (ASCA, 2005a). Individual short-term counseling that focuses on choices and consequences, solutions, and behavior change can help students understand what they need to do, how they need to do it, and measures of progress. Group counseling using a psycho-educational (i.e., structured, content-oriented) approach with students who have similar needs makes good use of time. Determining whether these services will be offered as open or closed groups, having scheduled meeting times, setting group rules, and using concrete measures of progress are good guidelines for psycho-educational counseling groups in general—and extremely important for students who have demonstrated challenges (e.g., social, emotional, behavioral) in the school environment but do not currently qualify for special education services.

Some students ineligible for special education support may receive classroom accommodations via a Section 504 plan. See Chapter 7 for a discussion of protections provided to students with disabilities under the Americans With Disabilities Act Amendments Act.

Supporting Parents and Families

Parent consultation can be on an individual and/or group basis. Families of students who qualify for special education services may need assistance in dealing with the emotions of the child's struggles in school and the impact of a special education "label." Others may be daunted by the decision that the student does not qualify for special education services and may need assistance in understanding and exploring options for support. Parent education programs can be a good use of the counselor's time for sharing information and strategies as well as answering questions in small groups.

Summary

The school counselor's services for students include individual planning as well as responsive individual and group counseling. In some cases, school-based short-term counseling by the school counselor or another qualified professional (e.g., clinical social worker) is written into a student's IEP. Writing clear, concrete IEP goals and objectives is important to guide counseling support services and to monitor student progress. When students are not found eligible for special education services, school counselors are important team members in the collaborative consultation approach in supporting these students and parents. Chapter 5 takes a look at the role of school counselors in student behavior support. The school counselor is an important resource for general education students, special education students, teachers, parents, and other school staff.

Reflective Questions

- What is the school counselor's role when a student is found eligible for special education support?

- What is the school counselor's role when a student is found ineligible for special education support?

The Role
of the School Counselor
in Behavior Support

Promoting Positive School Behavior

Special Education Services

Role of the School Counselor

• Identification of appropriate instructional approaches and classroom interventions

• Participation in team development of IEP goals

• Development of Behavior Intervention Plans

• Collaborative consultation

• Advocacy

• Inclusion

• Transitions

• Accountability

• Understanding behavior issues of students with disabilities

• Providing behavior interventions to students

• Support for general education teachers in managing classroom behaviors

A Shared Vision of Special Education and School Counseling

One of the most challenging aspects of teaching 21st-century students is managing individual and classroom behavior so students can learn. Students today are affected by numerous psychological, social, emotional, and academic issues, any one of which may affect their participation in the mission of the school: to educate students to become positive and contributing members of society. Students of all ages must attend school; some when they are ready for the learning environment and anxious to learn, and others because the law requires their attendance. If students could leave their everyday concerns outside the school building, teachers would find teaching a relatively easy task with students accessible to learning at all times and graduating from high school ready to participate in 21st-century life; in this scenario, counselors could focus on helping students become responsible contributing adults.

Unfortunately, our complex world means that a number of students enter school with challenging behaviors requiring that educators deal with difficult issues before students even start the task of learning. In the real world, where inappropriate behavior can impact a student's readiness and ability to learn, the school counselor frequently participates in tasks relating to mental health issues and behavior support.

Support for Students With Challenging Behaviors

Students with disabilities can exhibit some of the most challenging behaviors faced by classroom teachers; often these behaviors are more severe and intense than the behavior of their typically developing peers. Classroom teachers often rely on school counselors to help manage behaviors that are disruptive to the learning process of an individual student, or to support students impacted by a peer's behavior. The school counselor becomes the "go-to" person for confused staff and upset students who want quick answers and failsafe solutions to difficult questions about inappropriate behavior. Some school counselors have previous classroom teaching experience that contributes to their understanding of behavior management. Even if they possess only a fundamental understanding, however, they must provide solutions for teachers grappling with the challenging behaviors exhibited by students with disabilities.

The nature of behavior issues that surround or stem from a disability often compel both the classroom teacher and the school counselor to assume the role of behavior management specialists. In particular, school counselors may be asked to (a) model behavior management techniques in the classroom, (b) write a behavior intervention plan (BIP), (c) discuss behavior interventions and/or staff concerns with parents, or (d) provide answers for teachers frustrated by student behaviors that are beyond those encountered in everyday classroom situations. Counselors may be asked to participate in procedures that result in consequences outside the classroom or be part of a manifest determination review team that evaluates disciplinary actions relating to students with disabilities (see Chapter 3). School counselors may work in the classroom with teachers and students, or provide short-term counseling to students. They lead classroom guidance lessons about appropriate behaviors and social skills, and they participate on schoolwide student assistance teams (see Chapter 3). They function as an advocate for the student engaging in inappropriate behavior, and act as a buffer to counter the heightened emotions of staff members. In a study of 100 school counselors, from 75% to 83% of respondents reported involvement in behavior management issues, such as assisting with BIPs (Milsom, 2002).

The roles of a school counselor working with special education students are varied and require a comprehensive understanding of the behaviors typically associated with different types of disabilities, behavior management techniques, and methods of supporting other students (and teachers) impacted by the behavior. What exactly is the role of the school counselor in supporting behavior management for students with disabilities? How has the school counselor's role changed in response to current stressors in the world? What kind of behavior management skills are required to work with students with disabilities? These issues are best explored through a framework of understanding the mental health needs of students, the behavioral characteristics of students with disabilities, and the requirements of the school counseling program.

Student Response to Real-World Stressors

Every day family, cultural, environmental, economic, social, and emotional situations impact students' participation in the rigors of the educational process. Life's trauma and upheaval weigh heavily on students of any age. Stressful situations can be temporary or longterm, and include divorce or separation of parents, loss of a loved one, military deployment, mental health and emotional disorders, psychological and family difficulties, disabilities, parent's loss of employment, home foreclosure and homelessness, natural disaster, sexual abuse and violence, bullying, and drug and alcohol abuse.

Showing up for school, staying at school, and "learning" are not the same. In the educational setting, students' actions reflect the greater totality of their lives. At this crucial juncture, school counselors often become the linchpin that holds their educational system together while offering support and guidance.

The Foundation for Child Development (FCD) has tracked a combination of indicators of child well being since 1975. The 2010 report, which used the composite Child and Youth Well-Being Index (CWI), traced the consequences of recent economic recessions.

> The worst has yet to come. Our research shows that conditions for children deteriorated through 2009 and are projected to bottom out in 2010. Virtually all the progress made in the family economic well-being domain since 1975 will be wiped out. (FCD, 2010, p. 4)

The statistics mentioned in the report reflect a bleak picture. The percentage of children living below the poverty line was expected to peak at 21% in 2010, the highest rate of child poverty in 20 years (FCD, 2010), and

> The percentage of children living in families with no secure parental employment . . . will increase from 22 percent in 2006 to 26 percent in 2010. . . . For all families, the median annual family income is expected to decline. . . . The percent of children living in food-insecure households [is expected] to climb from 16.9 percent in 2007 to 17.7 percent in 2010 (FCD, 2010, p. 4). Children's overall health is expected to decline due to obesity (FCD, 2010, p. 5).

For students with disabilities, such conditions may make an already challenging life more susceptible to the vagaries of the economic recession and subsequent decline of a comfortable standard of living. Mental health needs may go unmet as local governments eliminate or reduce a variety of services, and educational school systems cut back in services and personnel.

Student Mental Health Issues

In spite of the complex economic realities that impact educational and mental health services, students still need support. In many instances, support is given through school resources. In November 2005, the Substance Abuse and Mental Health Services Administration (SAMHSA) issued a report based on its national survey of school mental health services during 2002–2003 (Foster et al., 2005). The researchers' review of literature from the previous 10 years "revealed that many children with mental health conditions do not receive any services and 70–80% of those who do, receive services from school-based providers" (p. 1). These school-based providers include school counselors, psychologists, and social workers. SAMHSA also developed the first national study of school mental health services, a survey based on two questionnaires sent to a nationally representative random sample of 2,125 K–12 public schools and 1,595 associated districts. From a response rate of 60%, survey results indicated that schools most frequently reported social, interpersonal, or family problems as the mental health category using the most resources; approximately 20% of schools reported that aggressive and disruptive behaviors required the most resources (Foster et al., 2005, Exhibit 22, p. 16). Short-term services provided included assessment, behavior management consultation, crisis intervention, referrals, individual and group counseling, and case management.

The *U.S. Surgeon General's Report on Children's Mental Health* (U.S. Department of Health and Human Services, 2000) reported that during any given year, one out of five children and adolescents experiences the signs and symptoms of a diagnosable mental health disorder. "Mental health disorders do not discriminate and their accompanying challenges can be found in families across all ethnic, socioeconomic, and educational backgrounds" (p. 56). In 2010, a National Institutes of Mental Health study analyzing data from the National Comorbidity Study-Adolescent Supplement that surveyed 10,000 U.S. teens (Merikangas et al., 2010), found that "fifty-one percent of boys and 49 percent of girls aged 13–19 have a mood, behavior, anxiety or substance use disorder. . . . In 22.2 percent of teens, the disorder was so severe it impaired their daily activities and caused great distress" (¶2–3).

Although a national issue, an additional threat to students with disabilities comes from the issue of bullying. Because of their special needs, "the cruel culture of teasing, bullying, and harassment that exists in the schools is particularly relevant for students with disabilities" (Schoen & Schoen, 2010, p. 68). Bullying occurs across a variety of disability types (Mishna, 2003). A study of students with mild disabilities found that they were more likely to be viewed as bullies by peers and perceived by teachers as being more likely to be victims of bullying than general education students (Estell et al., 2009). School counselors, with their unique communication and leadership skills, should be prepared to "assume responsibility and leadership in bullying reduction" (Bauman, 2008, p. 369).

Given the complexity of disabilities found in current inclusive education settings, it should be no surprise that students with disabilities often have mental health, social, and emotional issues that are transferred to the classroom. Such issues reflect the complex nature of disabilities resulting in behavioral implications requiring additional student support from resources such as the classroom teacher or the school counselor.

Mental Health Issues of Students With Disabilities

Most students with disabilities are served in their base, or neighborhood, school (U.S. Department of Education, 2010). Indicator 24 of *The Condition of Education 2010* report notes that "some 12 percent of students in public elementary schools had an Individualized Education Program (IEP)" (U.S. Department of Education, 2010, p. 82). These students receive related services through their IEP and are a part of the general and special education support structures in the school. Along with offering counseling as a related service, "school counselors are now being held responsible for providing preventative and supportive services for students with disabilities who are included in regular public school classes" (Bowen & Glenn, 1998, ¶1). The support role of school counselors requires a large amount of flexibility and a high degree of professional skill to contribute to the positive growth of students with disabilities.

School counselors support inclusive practices by providing students with disabilities the skills to participate in general education settings. Wagner, Newman, and Cameto (2004), looking at the related services provided to students with disabilities by or through school, found that the school experiences of students with disabilities in middle and high school have changed, requiring more mental health services. In order to help students function in their daily lives and in school, "the related services provisions of the Individuals With Disabilities Education Act (IDEA, 2006) make schools a major provider of health-related adaptive, social, emotional and technological support for students with disabilities" (Wagner et al., 2004, p. 3-7). Mental health services showed the largest increase (seven percentage points), with one out of five students receiving mental health services through their school. The largest growth in this type of service was in the category of students with emotional disturbance.

Today's School Counselor

An important part of counseling is assisting students to make decisions that result in a change to more effective behaviors. If the school counselor can coach students in school success skills in the classroom with regard to organization, listening and responding in appropriate ways, cooperating with peers, and completing class work and homework in a timely manner, they are more likely to experience success in these areas that can reinforce the application and reoccurrence of these new behaviors. Even with older students, the opportunity to practice new skills, even if cognitively understood in an individual counseling session, can be beneficial to making these skills a part of a new repertoire of behavior. (Clark & Breman, 2009, pp. 9–10)

Inclusive Practices

Inclusive classrooms that serve a wide range of students with disabilities means that the characteristics related to a disability are part of the classroom composition. Because the influence of these issues can impact students' ability to participate in the educational process, to some extent and (perhaps) contrary to the American School Counselor Association (ASCA) National Model (2005a), school counselors are often thrust into the business of providing behavior support for students both with and without disabilities; "when considering discipline, counseling students who have discipline problems is the role of the school counselor while performing the disciplinary action itself is the role of the administrator" (p. 57). One challenge for school counselors is defining their role in behavior support without being directly involved in student discipline.

The School Counselor's Role in Behavior Support

The school counselor is one of many educational resources that work together to promote a safe and positive school environment for all students. The school counselor serves as a resource for both students and teachers, functioning inside and outside the classroom to provide behavior support for students with disabilities (see Figure 5.1). Issues that place stress on the student, elicit concern from the teacher, and perhaps result in inappropriate behavior can be alleviated through internal school support and connection with outside resources.

Support in the Classroom

When teachers or administrators request behavioral support from the school counselor, different choices exist: staying in the classroom alongside the student or removing the student from the classroom. Intervening with the behavior in the setting in which it occurred (i.e., the classroom) enables the counselor to model appropriate behavior strategies for the teacher and other students,

Figure 5.1   Assisting Students With Disabilities With Behavior Issues

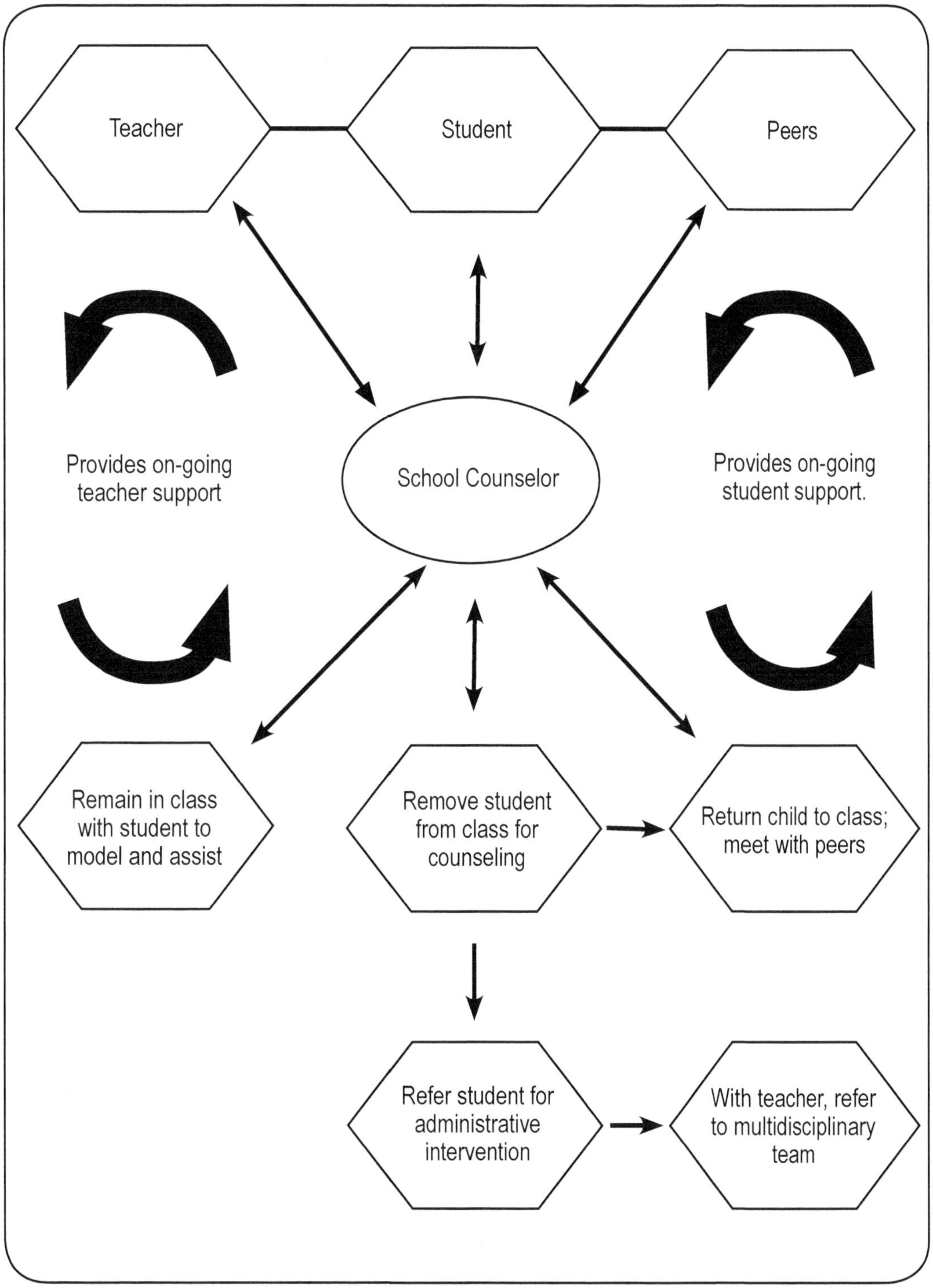

provide behavior cues for the student, validate that the student is part of the class, and promote peer acceptance. Offering support within the classroom allows the disruptive student to continue to be a participating member of ongoing academic activities while learning more acceptable behaviors.

Support for the Teacher

In addition to providing students with emotional support, school counselors also act as consultants to their colleagues. Classroom teachers manage behavior and instruct students at the same time, but consistent, chronic, and difficult behavior challenges influence their ability to teach while maintaining order. In writing about first-year special education teachers, Regan (2009) noted that "well-qualified teachers enter the classroom believing that all students should be valued, can learn, and have an innate need to belong," but when the behavior management tools they've learned "fail to demonstrate any success . . ., teachers may feel inadequate, incompetent, and helpless" (p. 61). Students with disabilities, whose behaviors may differ from those of their peers in both quantity and quality, can negatively affect the classroom teacher. Feelings of guilt, anger, or frustration stemming from the inappropriate behaviors may have an effect on teachers' relationships with students and, thus, impact their ability to fulfill professional responsibilities.

The classroom teacher, by constantly being subjected to inappropriate behavior, may be apprehensive about having the student with a behavior issue return to class. It is taxing for the classroom teacher to deal with difficult behavioral situations while simultaneously instructing students and maintaining other duties. The school counselor can support classroom teachers by listening to their concerns, providing them an opportunity to vent their discomfort, offering possible solutions, and maintaining a continuous interest in the ongoing progress of the student by checking periodically with the teacher. "Any individual who interacts with a student is a resource. When defeat feels just around the corner and the teacher has tried everything to engage the child, communicating with [a counselor] may bring new insight into the situation" (Regan, 2009, p. 64).

Support for the Student Outside the Classroom

When disruptive behaviors impact the entire class, however, and make learning hard, one behavior management strategy used by teachers is to control behaviors within the classroom as long as possible and then either "send the student to the counselor" or ask for the student to be removed. The school counselor in consultation with the classroom teacher can help determine if the inappropriate behavior is too disruptive for the student to remain in class. Perhaps the behavior has been displayed for a substantial amount of time or school policy dictates immediate removal for certain infractions (e.g., name-calling). Removal from the classroom provides an opportunity for the student to strategize alternative coping methods away from the setting in which the behavior occurred. Time with the student is spent defusing a tense situation, de-escalating or deflecting the behavior, calming the student, walking through the issues, processing the student's feelings, exploring more appropriate behaviors, sending them back to class ready to learn, and then communicating with the teacher about the outcome of the intervention.

For many students, immediate behavioral interventions work: students state their concerns, identify their behaviors, discuss appropriate ways of handling inappropriate behavior, practice different behavior strategies, and then return to class calm. The school counselor verbally walks through or role-plays with the student their reentry into the classroom and helps them anticipate concerns that may arise when the door opens and they return to class.

Support for Peers of the Student

In other situations, the transition back to class after removal for behavior issues requires more intense intervention from the school counselor. Students left behind in the classroom may not be delighted to see their peer come back. The inappropriate behavior of one student can affect the rhythm of teaching, and produce ambivalent feelings in other students, who might have experienced relief when the student was removed from their classroom. These students may need time to accept their peer's return. To make the transition back to the classroom easier for all students, the school counselor can work with the individual students who bore the brunt of the misbehavior, or work with the whole class by modeling appropriate greetings or suggesting ways to help the student reenter the classroom and feel a part of the group.

Counseling Students With Disabilities

Identifying Behaviors Associated With a Disability

Students with disabilities sometimes exhibit frustration when they recognize that they are "different" from their peers, and they may struggle to keep up with the constant flow of academic information in the educational setting. Students with learning disabilities may find certain teachers do not accommodate to their learning style, whereas students with attention disorders may lose the ability to focus and, in an effort to catch up, exhibit inappropriate behavior (e.g., calling out repeatedly, jumping out of seat).

Special education teachers often assist general education classroom teachers by identifying appropriate instructional approaches and interventions to support these students. School counselors, similarly, can support classroom teachers with their specific skill set and training, and can help defuse stressful situations. Supplementing the IDEA definitions of disabilities included in Appendix A, Table 5.1 provides a primer on some unique characteristics of different disabilities, typical classroom interventions, and how the school counselor can assist these students. Counselors should be aware that there are commonalities or similarities of characteristics across disabilities, however, and that many disabilities present a continuum of behaviors, from mild to severe. Some student actions may be a reflection of a disability and not necessarily intentional behavior.

Short-Term Counseling Approaches

All students, including those with disabilities, experience situations that require short-term counseling. Students with disabilities may not be able to cope adequately, may not be resilient or flexible, or may not have the skills or strategies to draw on when needed. Sometimes a disability limits the student's capacity to deal effectively with everyday issues, or the disability may be the catalyst that triggers the need for crisis counseling. Counseling students with disabilities who have behavior issues requires an objective approach, using questions and phrases that are not confrontational and recognizing their strengths, challenges, and perceptions (see Table 5.2).

Behavioral Interventions

Targeting the Right Behavior (or Knowing Which One to Change)

At times, more than one behavior may interfere with a student's ability to learn. The school counselor, in consultation with the teacher, needs to identify the behavior that is the most disorderly, and the one that if corrected or modified would allow the student to return to the

Table 5.1   School Counseling Program Support for Students With Disabilities

Characteristics of a student with ...	May include ...	Typical classroom interventions may include ...	School counseling program support might include ...
Autism spectrum disorder	Does not respond predictably to instructions, transitions, or requests Often solitary; misinterprets social cues Difficulty modulating voice Difficulty beginning, maintaining, and ending conversations Prefers routines	Preparation for activity changes; individual schedules Visual aids/graphic organizers Peer buddies/peer tutors who have been trained Shortened verbal requests	Demonstrating social interactions and facilitating group work Modeling appropriate tone of voice and response Helping to teach alternative behaviors and expand repertoire of likes/dislikes Teaching perspective and turn taking Discussing student's interest to build social skills in a group setting
Attention deficit hyperactivity disorder (included in IDEA category "other health impairment")	Inattention; lack of impulse control Difficulty finishing work Makes choices not in his or her best interest	Incorporate time for physical movement in daily schedule Time management tools (e.g., timer) Break tasks into manageable units; clear due dates for short- and long-term assignments Written or graphic organizers	Providing consistent behavior supports; reinforcing appropriate behaviors Offering psychoeducation groups to help students prioritize work, develop self-monitoring checklists, learn to break assignments into units/steps
Blind and/or visual impairment	Slow processing of content/response Disoriented Delayed language development Stereotypic behaviors (e.g., head weaving)	Instruction incorporates concrete materials and objects; multimodal/experiential approach Tactile/verbal cues Explicit directions Braille Large print materials Orientation and mobility instruction	Modeling interactions for classmates and other adults (e.g., identify self when answering or asking questions) Providing psychoeducational group and one-on-one opportunities to practice metacognitive strategies

Table 5.1   School Counseling Program Support for Students With Disabilities (cont'd)

Characteristics of a student with ...	May include ...	Typical classroom interventions may include ...	School counseling program support might include ...
Deaf and hard of hearing	Isolated from peers Frequent requests for directions to be repeated Difficulty following verbal directions Written language that reflects absence of appropriate syntax Difficulty communicating with others	Peer buddies who have basic signing skills Visual, illustrations, diagrams, models, pictures Assistive technology/multimedia Augmentative communication system Multimedia approach	Setting up buddy system for peer helpers Assisting students to develop a portfolio to highlight social successes Providing information to staff about disability and assistance that can be helpful to students and teachers
Developmental delay	Difficulty maintaining attention Frustration with tasks Delays in speech and language, fine/gross motor skills, and/or personal/social skills Difficulty playing/associating with peers	Limit variety of activities Use picture schedules, sequence activities, establish routines Break tasks into manageable units Use songs or rhymes to reinforce information Support tasks with movement	Using drama and role-playing to teach problem solving Acknowledging effort and progress through positive reinforcement Promoting choices to foster positive social interactions
Emotional or behavioral disorder	"Externalizers" may be aggressive, disruptive, or act out "Internalizers" may be withdrawn, anxious, or depressed Inadequate coping skills Choosing dangerous or inappropriate playmates/friends Difficulty maintaining positive, productive relationships	Break tasks into manageable units Peer buddies/peer mentors who are trained Offer choices for assignments Materials aligned to student's instructional level	Offering to mediate interactions with peers and suggest/model how to compromise Teaching and providing opportunities to practice self-regulation skills Teaching problem-solving and coping skills Providing groups for social skill-building

Table 5.1   School Counseling Program Support for Students With Disabilities (cont'd)

Characteristics of a student with ...	May include ...	Typical classroom interventions may include ...	School counseling program support might include ...
Intellectual disability	Inadequate understanding of social cues Difficulty processing content and expressing ideas "Learned helplessness" Difficulty making friends	Visual and verbal cues Step-by-step instruction; acronyms to remember information Graphic organizers and/or written instructions Peer tutors	Modeling and providing opportunities to practice appropriate social skills Teaching skills for studying and strategies for learning Teaching problem-solving skills
Learning disability	Difficulty understanding social cues TOO negative. Difficulty following verbal or written directions Demonstrates competencies in many areas but does not acquire academic skills without great effort Misinterprets social skills	Students repeat/paraphrase directions Peer tutors Mnemonics to remember instructions Graphic organizers/visual aids/written instructions Extended time on assignments, tests Break tasks into manageable units Lesson delivery through multiple formats including technology	Coordinating peer-tutoring program Teaching, monitoring, and practicing social skills in a small group Teaching self-monitoring devices
Multiple disabilities	Difficulty managing unstructured time Difficulty with social interactions Lack of understanding of time andscheduling	Choices in preplanned activities and assignments Visual cues for appropriate activities during unstructured time Daily schedule posted	Offering psychoeducational groups to present social stories to understand appropriate interactions Assisting in choice-making activities

Table 5.1   School Counseling Program Support for Students With Disabilities (cont'd)

Characteristics of a student with ...	May include ...	Typical classroom interventions may include ...	School counseling program support might include ...
Physical disabilities and/or orthopedic impairment	Sensory input needs Incomplete work, difficulty focusing on activity Needs extended time to learn Profits from revisiting early learning before new information presented	Adaptive equipment, sensory aids (e.g., weighted vest) Visual aids, labels, place markers Break tasks into manageable units; use time-management tools (e.g., timer)	Providing out of classroom sensory breaks Providing opportunities to practice problem-solving skills with application to real life
Speech/language disorder	Difficulty with pragmatic language, articulation, composing full sentences Difficulty conversing with peers which may affect social relationships	Give student "think time" Visual aids/concrete examples in instruction Offer ways of presenting information that do not require lengthy oral expression	Providing opportunities to model and practice social and communication skills Offering psychoeducational groups with a focus on social skills Coordinating peer collaboration opportunities and after-school or community projects
Traumatic brain injury	Poor impulse control Agitation and irritation Lowered social inhibitors	Visual aids, labels, checklists Assistive technology Extended time to complete assignments	Providing opportunities to model and practice self-regulation skills (e.g., deep breathing, positive self-talk) Assisting with implementation of "memory notebook"

Note. The characteristics noted in this table likely occur in all children from time to time. When they are manifestations of a disability, they occur along a continuum of severity and are marked by longer duration and higher frequency. See Appendix A for IDEA definitions of these disability categories.

classroom. Generally, this behavior is the one that is the most disruptive to the flow of the educational process. For example, a student may choose to sit quietly rather than follow directions and participate in a group activity; this behavior, although not desired, is not disruptive to the rest of the class. For a student with disabilities, personal discord can take a variety of outward manifestations. Challenging and verbally aggressive behaviors are usually those that are the most unsettling and are of immediate concern. The following section discusses developing specific plans for students exhibiting more concerning behaviors, to address the reasons for their actions and support them in developing alternative, socially acceptable behaviors.

Behavior Intervention Plans (BIPs)

Even after short-term counseling and other approaches have been employed, some students require more intensive behavior interventions. BIPs are one method of providing assistance to the student to modify or increase appropriate behavior. A classroom teacher may request the assistance of the school counselor in writing the behavior plan or ask for help in setting up a meeting with other specialists to discuss the inappropriate behavior and to brainstorm possibilities for behavior changes. The school counselor also can facilitate the discussion that leads to a BIP. Each school counselor can access a variety of resources to assist them in writing behavior intervention plans (see, e.g., Baditoi, 2010).

Student Contracts. Student contracts are often written with the school counselor as a type of positive reinforcement for the student. Because of a somewhat flexible schedule, school counselors are able to provide primary or secondary reinforcers for students with behavior contracts. However, involvement in both behavior management support and positive reinforcement can put school counselors in a difficult position if they are both managing behavior with school staff and delivering the positive reinforcement.

Student Self-Monitoring, Self-Talk, and Self-Reinforcement. Other strategies for self-management include teaching students self-management tools. These individual strategies promote awareness and independence and are positive methods for students with disabilities to identify and use in learning how to modify their own behavior.

Table 5.2   Counseling Students With Disabilities Regarding Behavior Issues

Do You Do This?

1. Use objective terms to describe the behavior?

2. Let the student know you care and want to help?

3. Use validated data?

4. Describe interactions with peers and adults objectively, not just repeating what others have said?

5. View the whole child?

6. Summarize student strengths?

7. Acknowledge student weaknesses?

8. Identify areas of concern for the student and class?

9. Process alternative behaviors?

10. Explain disciplinary consequences if needed?

11. Return the student to the class room calm, ready to work, and understanding the appropriate ways to handle the problem if it recurs?

Try not to say this:

> Mrs. Smith says you don't work, and you are not nice to the other students. She wishes you were not in her class. Do you know the other students in the classroom don't want to work and play with you?

Instead, say this:

> Mrs. Smith says you are having trouble today in class. Can you tell me what is happening? I know your teacher and classmates want you to be with them, so we need to work on appropriate behavior so you can return to class and stay there.

The Role of the School Counselor in Positive Behavior Support (PBS)

The RTI (response to intervention) approach has been researched for many years in literacy and more recently in math. For almost 30 years, the process has facilitated the use of positive behavioral interventions and supports (Office of Special Education Programs, n.d.-b). IDEA legislation and regulations mirror RTI language in advising states how to identify students with possible learning disabilities. The roles a counselor may play in behavior intervention in each of the tiers, and during the referral and eligibility process for special education, are flexible and dependent on school and district policies.

In an RTI approach to behavior (Figure 5.2; Trussel, 2008, p. 180), Tier 1 provides schoolwide programs, such as violence prevention, school behavior expectations, conflict resolution, and social skills programs. Approximately 80% of the student body should respond to this level of prevention (Horner & Sugai, 2000). Approximately 10% to 15% (Horner & Sugai, 2000) of students do not respond to Tier 1 programs and require secondary supports in Tier 2, such as study and supplemental academic skills, increased social skills and self-management training, cognitive behavioral interventions, and counseling. Tier 3 is the final level of support for students who do not respond to Tiers 1 and 2 (approximately 3%-5% of students from Tier 2) and may need more intensive supports and alternatives to suspension and expulsion such as individual behavior management plans. Counselors in this model (a) become a safe haven for the student exhibiting emotional and behavioral challenges, (b) provide supportive crisis intervention services, (c) continually monitor the student's adjustment and emotional status, and (d) provide an opportunity to practice previously introduced social and problem-solving skills (Pearce, 2009).

Functional Behavior Assessment (FBA)

Some students with disabilities require a more rigorous approach to behavior interventions. As mentioned previously, IDEA requires that school teams must use an FBA when disciplinary actions for problem behaviors may result in a more restrictive environment and when those behaviors are a manifestation of the student's disability (34 CFR § 300.350[f]). The FBA process requires teams to observe and analyze the behavior to determine the antecedent, behavior, and consequences; implementing the process proactively leads to the development of behavior interventions and supports to include in the student's IEP, and may reduce or prevent behavior problems by suggesting alternative behaviors for students to use.

Figure 5.2   Positive Behavior Support in RTI Model

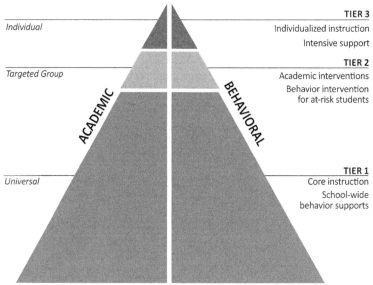

SOURCE: "Response to Intervention: Policy Considerations and Implementation,"
National Association of State Directors of Special Education, 2005

Tier 1	Tier 2	Tier 3
(Primary; 80%–85% of students)	(Secondary; 10%–15% of students from Tier 1 receive targeted group assistance, explicit instruction, and intense supports targeted to skill deficits)	(Tertiary; 3%–5% of students from Tier 2)
• Universal screening • Scientifically based instruction • Ongoing progress monitoring • General education teachers and staff • RTI Team member • Provides interventions • Assesses data • Assists with ongoing process • Guides parents through RTI process • May facilitate team	• Intensive social skills teaching and support • Self-management programs • School-based adult mentors • Increased academic support • Practice and/or alternatives to out-of-school suspension	• Universal behavioral supports • Effective academic support • Social skills teaching • Teaching school behavior expectations • Active supervision and monitoring in common areas • Positive reinforcement for students • Consistent and fair corrective discipline and effective classroom management

Summary

The school counselor is an important resource for students with disabilities facing negative outcomes of their behavior. School counselors do more than simply offer support for students and staff; their objective encouragement validates the feelings of educators and students, promotes positive academic achievement, and facilitates social and emotional growth and development.

As students with disabilities mature and reach postsecondary age, the school counselor remains involved. Chapter 6 provides an overview of educational transitions, in particular issues related to postsecondary transitions through the lens of continuous and related counseling services for special education students.

Reflective Questions

- What is the role of the school counselor in the behavior management of students with disabilities?

- How do school counselors ensure that they are kept "in the loop" when special education students are involved in behavior and discipline issues?

Providing Transition Services for Students With Disabilities

Special Education Services

Role of School Counselor

- Development of appropriate IEP transition goals

- Programming for self-advocacy, social, and academic goals

- Monitoring of progress toward postsecondary education, career, and vocational goals

- Collaborative consultation
- Advocacy
- Inclusion
- Transitions
- Accountability

- Support for students and parents with transitions

- Advocacy for students and parents in accessing appropriate school and community resources

- Resource for postsecondary planning

A Shared Vision of Special Education and School Counseling

Students are faced with a number of transitions as they navigate their school years. Transitions can be *vertical* (i.e., sequential and over time, grade to grade, school to school) and *horizontal* (i.e., moving between classrooms), both of which can create challenges for students with disabilities (Milsom, 2007). Each year approximately 27% of 15- to 16-year-old students receiving special education services drop out of school (Frasier, 2007). Effective transition programs can decrease negative effects (e.g., dropping out) and increase academic achievement. Effective transition programs include *bridging activities* that provide information, social support to the student in planning the transition, and collaboration with both educators and parents (Akos & Galassi, 2004; Mizelle & Irvin, 2000).

Using the ecological perspective (see Chapter 3), school transitions for students with disabilities can be understood within a social system with particular focus on the micro and meso components over time. Students' individual relationships with others—such as family members, friends, and classmates—are the microsystems. The interactions between and among the microsystems are the mesosystems. More open and supportive mesosystems generate more positive outcomes for students. Regular communication, agreement on expectations, and preparation for new environments results in transitions being a process rather than an event (Milsom, 2007).

School counselors support the transition process for students with disabilities in many ways, and the process must start early and be ongoing. The transition component should address the academic, career, and personal/social development needs of students transitioning into kindergarten, middle school, and high school, and then transitioning into postsecondary life. Students with disabilities are supported by a collaborative consultation team approach as they maneuver these transitions, from the beginning of their formal education to the beginning of their postsecondary pursuits.

Transitioning Into Kindergarten

There is a distinct developmental shift for children as they transition into the formal school setting of kindergarten. This shift can be particularly stressful for students with disabilities and their parents. The transition to kindergarten includes increased independence and responsibility; social networks that change from those primarily with adults to those with peers; and the cognitive challenges of language, writing, and number skills. It's not just the students who are transitioning; their parents are transitioning as well. Parents may have concerns about whether their child will socially adjust to the classroom environment and if their child's "specialness" will be understood and appreciated (Augst & Akos, 2009).

Kindergarten transition programs have been shown to have positive effects for both students and parents (Schulting, Malone, & Dodge, 2006). Using the collaborative consultation model, school counselors can (a) articulate a well-defined and forward-looking purpose for the successful transition of students with special needs into kindergarten, (b) write goals that link purpose to outcomes, (c) provide the leadership and advocacy to connect students with special needs and their families with school personnel, (d) maintain communication to share ideas and information, (e) facilitate a sense of camaraderie and involvement through working together, and (f) maintain high levels of mutual respect (Michan & Rodger, 2005). Kindergarten transition programs may include the following (Augst & Akos, 2009):

- Small group tours of the school for students and their parents. Ask older students (e.g., fifth-graders) to serve as student ambassadors to incoming kindergarten students. Ask parents to be their child's aide during the session. Invite various school personnel (e.g., principal, teachers, school psychologist, school nurse, cafeteria workers) to participate.

- Breakfast sessions hosted by the school counselor to provide information to parents.

- Group counseling to reinforce social skills and behavioral interventions for selected kindergarten students.

- Classroom guidance to introduce and reinforce appropriate social skills for all kindergarten students.

- Newsletters to provide information and resources to parents.

Transitioning From Elementary to Middle School

The transition from elementary to middle school is one of the most significant for students with disabilities (Carter, Clark, Cushing, & Kennedy, 2005; Milsom, 2007). Unfortunately, many students never recover from a stressful or unsuccessful transition to middle school (Carter et al., 2005), and this can be reflected in difficulties in both academic and personal arenas. Of concern will be the widening achievement gap in math and science between students with and without disabilities (Milsom, 2007).

Working as a collaborative team, school counselors from both the elementary school and the middle school are the mesosystem catalyst to open communication, to encourage information sharing, and to develop clearly defined expectations for students and families as part of the transition process. Individual student planning through small-group advisement as well as individual and group counseling provides opportunities for students to develop self-awareness (e.g., interests, skills, abilities) so they can begin to develop self-advocacy skills. It is important for students to be able to learn about and practice social, organizational, and study skills, and how to be appropriately assertive. Developing these skills will be beneficial for students with disabilities during the vertical transition from elementary to middle school as well as the new experience of transitioning between classrooms and among various teachers.

The Transition IEP Meeting

During the IEP meeting, the collaborative consultation team may include elementary and middle school counselors, special education teachers, parents, support personnel (e.g., school psychologist), and, when appropriate, the special education student who can reflect on his or her elementary school experiences. This is an opportunity to identify supports that have been successful (and which have not), instructional strategies that have been effective (and which have not), and student preferences (e.g., learning style, interests) based on the elementary school experience (Carter et al., 2005). This is also a good time to begin thinking about the future so that a meaningful middle school experience can be planned. The school experience will comprise both academic and extracurricular activities. During planning meetings, existing successful supports, strategies, and preferences can be incorporated into the student's middle school IEP (see end of chapter for a blank form that can be used to collect this information).

Transition Activities

Transition activities should begin in the spring for both students and parents. Orientation activities and open houses are options for providing information about and demonstrations of the variety of curricular and extracurricular activities that are offered at the middle school. Student ambassadors (i.e., older middle school students) can host special education students for a school event (e.g., basketball game, spaghetti dinner, band concert) and at an open house while parents meet with school personnel. School counselors can schedule small group meetings with parents so that questions can be answered and concerns can be discussed. These initial contacts with parents should be maintained to keep the lines of communication open. By maintaining communication, school counselors can receive feedback from parents about the effectiveness of the transition activities.

Collaboration and teaming among elementary and middle school counselors and other support personnel to plan and schedule transition activities may include the following (Akos, 2002; Carter et al., 2005):

Spring before transition to middle school:

- Generate list of students with disabilities who will be transitioning to respective middle schools.

- Collaborative consultation team (e.g., school counselors, special education teachers, support personnel) meets to discuss transition activities.

- Complete IEP meetings.

- Students and parents visit middle school, meet with school counselors and special education teachers.

Summer orientation:

- Practice changing classrooms, opening lockers; eat in cafeteria.

- Classroom guidance programs on study skills; choices, responsibility, and consequences related to school discipline; social skills and student conduct.

- Introduction to student activities (e.g., athletics, music, clubs).

- Review of academic and career plans, course scheduling.

Fall follow-up:

- **With parents**, meetings to provide information, answer questions, evaluate transition activities.

- **With students**, small-group advisement to review transition experience, academic progress, extracurricular activities; group counseling to reinforce appropriate social skills, test-taking strategies; individual counseling as needed for next cycle.

- **With members of collaborative consultation team,** evaluate pretransition activities and success of student transitions; formulate recommendations.

Transitioning From Middle School to High School

Many students feel trepidation over the transition to high school. A new building, new schedule, and new teachers along with more students and more opportunities to become lost seems a disaster about to happen for many students with disabilities. However, with caring and thoughtful planning on the school counselor's part, using supportive individual student planning and advisement coupled with individual and group counseling, the middle-to-high school transition process can be positive (see Frasier, 2007; Milsom, 2007).

Once again, the collaborative consultation team involves school counselors, parents, special and general education teachers, other school personnel, community resources, and special education students. Building on past success with transition activities, identifying needs, and making a plan helps to ensure that the transition from middle school to high school is effective. Topics and skill areas helpful to the transitioning high school student include learning about and appreciating diversity, understanding their disability and how to self-advocate, developing skills (e.g., organization, test taking, studying), building positive social skills, and training in being assertive. It can be expected that the school counselor's activities will include classroom guidance, individual student planning and small-group advisement, and responsive services (collaborative consultation with parents, teachers, other school personnel, community resources; short-term individual counseling; group counseling). Table 6.1 provides some tips for school counselors on working with this population of students.

Focusing on Career Development

Career development can be a guiding force in middle school where exploration is encouraged. Activities developing career awareness can help students begin to set goals directed at postsecondary planning. Linking self-awareness with future career goals sets the foundation for courses to take in high school, clubs and sports participation, and a positive attitude towards learning. Mentors from the community, or even high school students who have dealt with similar disabilities, can be positive role models. It is important to begin planning for postsecondary opportunities as early as middle school (see Table 6.2).

Table 6.1   Top 10 Tips for Providing Transition Support Services

Tip #1: Start Early	Current practice and legal requirements (i.e., IDEA) stipulate that transition planning should be initiated as early as possible and no later than the age of 16. It is recommended, however, that students begin the process in middle school by participating in job fairs, being introduced to work-study programs, and attending Career Day events that help them to begin thinking about life after high school.
Tip #2: Identify a Goal	Assist the student in identifying goals that are specific and can be broken down into measurable steps. A good place to start is to ask the student to write a paragraph or record a short statement about "what do I do well?" and "what I want to do when I graduate from high school." Look for key words and phrases with which the student seems to personally identify and are not prefaced with "My mother says I should...." Once the goal has been stated in specific terms ("I want to go to college"), identify specific steps that need to be taken to achieve the goal. As a counselor, this is a good place to find out what the student does or does not know about what steps need to be taken. Along with the transition specialist and special educator, a plan can be developed to assist the student with gaining knowledge and completing each step.

Tip #3: Focus on Strengths	Students with disabilities need to understand their disability-specific issues so they can become powerful self-advocates. Each of us has a number of challenges and limitations, but we also need to know our strengths and capabilities. As counselors, we know how to do positive asset searches; use your counseling expertise to encourage and support students in being actively involved as self-advocates so they can understand their challenges and limitations as well as their strengths and capabilities to develop a lifestyle across all life roles. These life roles include relating to others, working either as a volunteer or an employee, managing life skills, having fun with extracurricular activities and avocational pursuits, and valuing what is important that will provide a meaningful lifestyle.

Tip #4: Resources	As school counselors, we need to remember this is a collaborative team approach and there are a variety of resources that can be utilized. There are people resources (e.g., teachers, parents, classmates), technology resources (e.g., computer-assisted guidance, web sites), and community resources (e.g., Vocational Rehabilitation, Junior Achievement, Boys/Girls Clubs, Scouts). Search your community to identify a variety of resources that you can call on as a part of the team.

Tip #5: Involve the Student	Unfortunately, oftentimes we do things "for students" and talk "about students"—of course with the very best of intentions. We need to involve students at appropriate times and in a developmental context that encourages them to understand disability-specific issues, to recognize strengths and capabilities, and to become active participants in their academic experience. Students with disabilities are provided self-advocacy training by the special education team, and counselors can be a source of support as well as an empathic encourager who knows when to appropriately challenge a student and when to offer positive reinforcement.
Tip #6: Involve the Parents 	Federal law as well as best practice mandates that parents be involved in their student's education. Some parents are well informed, some are overinvolved, some are overwhelmed, and some are unsure of how to allow their children to move on to independence. Part of the transition process is to help parents understand the possibilities for the future while at the same time to begin in earnest the process of letting go. Some parents have played an active part in the IEP process and have interfaced with school staff; they now will have to allow and assist their children to do it on their own.

Tip #7: **Be Culturally Sensitive**	There is an overrepresentation of minorities in special education. It is important for school counselors to find culturally sensitive approaches and be willing to challenge stereotypes so that students are provided with the services that are needed.
Tip #8: **Attend to Deadlines** 	Whether students are transitioning from middle school to high school or high school to postsecondary pursuits, deadlines are a critical part of the life journey. Missing a deadline can mean a student may lose out on an opportunity. Finding multiple ways to post reminders about deadlines will help students to know where to look for this important information. The school web page, school counselor's web page, e-mail, bulletin board, school newsletter, and personal reminders are just a few of the ways to post reminders.

Tip #9: Individualize the Services 	Caseloads for counselors seem to grow larger each year. Where can you find the time to meet the needs of each and every student? First, the collaborative team approach is one good way to muster the resources of many "experts" to best meet the needs of our special education students. Second, disaggregate your data so you can identify smaller groups of students that can benefit from your professional services through the school counseling program. Third, find a system for being able to keep track of the information on your caseload. Fourth, periodically review your caseload to be sure no one is "falling through the cracks." And finally, does every student on your caseload have a postsecondary plan?
Tip #10: Use a Collaborative Team 	Postsecondary planning for special education students requires a team approach. Work with special education teachers, transition specialists, classroom teachers, and administrators.

Table 6.2 Planning for Postsecondary Opportunities

Middle School	Students with disabilities should be active participants in IEP meetings.
	Students need to understand their strengths and challenges as well as how to develop strategies to be academically successful.
	Students should be developing an understanding of the way they learn.
	Students need to know how to use their learning style to be academically successful.
	Students need to be able to utilize study skills, time management, test preparation, and test-taking strategies that fit their learning needs to meet the benchmarks set to become a high school graduate.
	Students should take the most appropriate academic program in the most integrated setting.
	Students need opportunities for career exploration through speakers, field trips, computer-assisted exploration, volunteer/work experiences, and mentors
	Students identify interests and preferences that can be critical components in developing their high school course of study.
	Students need to develop independent decision-making skills and self-determination by setting goals at school and at home. These skills and motivations can be nurtured through being more actively involved in their IEP meetings.
High School	The goal of every student should be some type of postsecondary education (e.g., on-the-job training, apprenticeship, community college, college).
	Students with a disability need to
	understand their learning needs,
	understand their strengths and limitations, learn their rights under the law,
	select courses that will prepare them for postsecondary education, explore career options, and develop greater independence.
	Students need to understand the nature of one's disability and what the disability is and is not.
	Using proper terminology and not using a disability as an "excuse" will keep students on track not only while in school but also in their personal life and across their life span.
	Understanding one's disability enables the student to become a self-advocate and to focus on areas of academic strengths, athletic abilities, and creative talents.
	Students need to participate in extracurricular activities to broaden their horizons, develop confidence by being successful in an activity, and establish positive relationships.
	Students should focus on career development by completing interest inventories, checklists, rating scales, and journaling to concretely help with self-understanding.

Ongoing Transition Activities

Many of the same transition activities used from elementary school to middle school can be used for the transition from middle school to high school. In high school, there are more activities offered, more courses to choose from, more teachers to get to know, and more varied day-to-day schedules for students. This can be particularly challenging for students with disabilities. With the emphasis on academic achievement, many classroom teachers will be reluctant to release students from class to meet with the school counselor. High school counselors need to be creative in finding time to meet with students (e.g., before school, lunch time, after school). The services provided through the school counseling program should make a difference for students; demonstrated results for students with disabilities who participate in transition program activities can go a long way in helping teachers and other school personnel understand the importance of students participating in these activities.

The Postsecondary Transition

Although transitions occur throughout the student's school experience, postsecondary planning (e.g., college, training, apprenticeship, work) provides an important opportunity for school counselors to assist students with disabilities. Individuals With Disabilities Education Act (IDEA) legislation and regulations require transition planning with students beginning at age 16, and include discussing their transition out of high school and the choices available to them (34 CFR § 300.321[b]; 20 U.S.C. § 1414[d][1][B]). Although the case manager and special education team are responsible for ensuring that procedurally correct paperwork is completed for the student's IEP, the school counselor's input at this juncture is vital. Along with the special education team, the school counselor is a part of the transition IEP team and works with the student to help determine appropriate plans for the future.

The IEP team must discuss the student's academic and career future and determine appropriate steps to achieve the goals of a work environment or a college path by identifying postsecondary goals. IDEA defines secondary transition as "a coordinated set of activities designed to be within a results-oriented process, . . . focused on improving the academic and functional achievement of the [student] to facilitate . . . movement to post-school activities, including postsecondary education, vocational education, integrated employment . . . ; continuing and adult education, adult services, independent living, or community participation" and "is based on the individual child's needs, taking into account the child's strengths, preferences, and interests" (34 CFR 300.43[a]; 20 U.S.C. § 1412[a][15][A][iii]).

Some school districts have special education transition specialists who specifically work with special education students to develop their postsecondary plans. These specialists contact outside agencies and link the students to state and federal programs for which they may be eligible. The transition specialist may help the student find a job if the student plans on working or help with applications if job training, community college, or a 4-year college as the goal. School divisions that do not have transition specialists may rely on the school counselor to supply the information and target opportunities for postsecondary planning, keeping in mind that the goals are collaboratively written with the special education case manager and the IEP team.

Students have a variety of options for postsecondary education and training. It is important that the school counselor use a collaborative team approach with the student as he or she learns about these various opportunities. In most cases, the transition specialist will take the lead in assisting the student in finding further education and training opportunities. It is important to provide a structured approach that is arranged in manageable steps, which can be monitored to provide positive reinforcement throughout the process. Students and parents may need to know about such varied possibilities as options in higher education (e.g., college/university, community college), training (e.g., apprenticeship, on-the-job training), and independent living—and also about the student's rights and responsibilities in these different settings. Working with the IEP team, the school counselor provides additional information about employment, training, and college. School counselors may be asked to write letters of recommendation for employment, training, and other postsecondary opportunities. Because high school counselors may have more access to college materials, they can serve as the source for coordinating college visits, financial aid resources, and the college application process.

Postsecondary Higher Education Opportunities

Appropriate postsecondary and transitions planning for students with disabilities is the responsibility of the special education team. However, school counselors can take an active part as a collaborative team member by lending expertise in the areas of individual and group counseling services, psychoeducational programs, parent workshops, and coordinating the application process—particularly as they relate to higher education institutions (i.e., community colleges and universities). As student advocates, school counselors can work collaboratively with teachers and other professionals to create the conditions necessary for successful transition to further education (Milsom, 2007; Milsom & Dietz, 2009). The Delivery System and Accountability components of the school counseling program model (American School Counselor Association, 2005a) include responsibility for supporting students with disabilities in their exploration of postsecondary educational opportunities.

Disability Disclosure

Because there are laws (i.e., Section 504 of the Rehabilitation Act of 1973, Americans With Disabilities Act of 1990, and ADA Amendments Act of 2008) that do not allow college admissions offices to ask if a student has a disability, it is the student's choice whether to disclose that he/she has a disability. These laws also state that colleges cannot deny or reject an applicant only because the student has disclosed a disability. However, all students applying to a college must meet the admissions criteria that have been set, and this includes students with disabilities. It is important to note that college admissions committees do have some flexibility in the admissions process. Disclosing a disability may help provide the admissions committee with a context for the student's grades, test scores, activities, interests, and possible college major.

Disclosing a disability on the application form may make it easier for the student to connect with disability services at the college and to disclose the disability with professors once classes begin. If the student chooses not to disclose a disability, the student will not be eligible to receive accommodations. It is advisable for the student to contact the office for disability services at the college he or she is applying to and speak with someone about the advantages and disadvantages of disclosing a disability during the application process. Students need to be aware of their own responsibilities as well as their rights in the postsecondary education setting (see Table 6.3).

The School Counselor's Role in Postsecondary Education Planning

High school counselors have experience in the college search and admissions processes and can play a critical role in assisting students with disabilities to make the most of their postsecondary educational opportunities. Counselors understand student development and have the necessary skills to address a student's challenges with a strength-based approach. School counselors understand that "successful transition to college opens the door for future economic success, social power, and personal well-being" (Milsom & Hartley, 2005, p. 436). Also, school counselors are valued resources for students and parents: developing a relationship with admissions officers and understanding the unique services offered, they can help to identify the "best match" for students with disabilities.

Table 6.3   Differences Between High School and College

Rights and Responsibilities	High School	College
Your right to an education	Education is a right and must be provided. Attendance laws require presence.	You must go through an admissions process and meet the criteria to be admitted to the college.
Rights as a person with a disability	IDEA entitles you to special education services and accommodations for your disability.	The Americans With Disabilities Act and Section 504 provide some services and accommodations for individuals with disabilities.
Identification of a disability	The school is responsible for identifying your disability.	You are responsible for documenting your disability and requesting services.
Accommodations	Your IEP states the accommodations you are entitled to receive, and the school must provide these accommodations.	You must apply and request accommodations. Once the college approves the accommodations, you must arrange for the services through the disability services office and self-advocate with your professors.
Support	Teachers, parents, school counselors help you to make decisions.	You will need to ask for support and assistance from the disability services office.
Access to records and grades	Up to the age of 18, your parents can access your school grades and participate in IEP meetings.	After age 18, your parents cannot access your school records or grades without your written permission.
Class meeting times	Generally, classes meet every day and are between 45–90 minutes in length.	Classes may meet 1, 2, 3, or sometimes 4 tines each week; class sessions can range from 45 minutes to 3 hours. Your class schedule will change every term/semester.
Class location	Your classes meet in one or maybe two different buildings on one campus.	Your classes will meet in different buildings in different locations on the campus.
Contact with teachers	You usually see your teachers every day.	You will probably see your teachers only on the days you have class. You will need to make an appointment to see a teacher at another time.
Class size	Usually, your classes range from 25–30 students.	The students in a class can range from 30 to over 300 students.
Assignments	Teachers will remind you about assignments, due dates, and tests.	You are expected to check the course syllabus for assignments, grading criteria, and due dates.
Costs	If you attend a public school, it is free.	You are responsible for paying tuition and fees to attend college. If you need financial assistance, you are responsible for applying for financial aid.

Note: For more information, see HEATH Resource Center (n.d.), Parents' Guide to the Transition of Their Adult Child to College, Career, and Community.

Using the collaborative team approach, school counselors are an integral part of an effective team that shares the responsibility for the postsecondary educational opportunities transition plan. The team includes the student, parents, both general and special education teachers, and others who have a clear understanding of the roles and responsibilities on the team. The student should understand and be able to identify his or her needs and become a self-advocate to communicate these needs to others. Parents support these self-determination skills knowing that "personal and professional success is facilitated by development of self-advocacy skills" (Milsom & Hartley, 2005, p. 439).

Admissions Tests

Most colleges require a standardized admissions test, such as the ACT or the SAT. Students may need assistance in registering to take these tests and in requesting needed accommodations, such as tape-recorded versions, large block answer sheets, extended time, extra breaks, or a small-group testing setting. Students with documented disabilities must be approved for accommodations by the respective testing organization (ACT, see http://www.act.org/aap/disab/index.html; The College Board for SAT, see http://www.collegeboard.com/ssd/student/) prior to registering for the test. Applying for accommodations can take several weeks, so the process should be started well in advance of the testing date. However, once approved, students may receive these accommodations for any of the exams ACT and The College Board sponsor. Because it takes time to make appropriate arrangements at a testing site (e.g., proctor, space, materials), changes requested less than 2 weeks before a test date cannot be guaranteed until the next test date. Although the registration reflects the approved accommodations that the student will receive at the test site, the test report will not disclose the details about these accommodations.

Letters of Recommendation for College Applications

Based on data from college admission and enrollment statistics, the most important criteria in admissions decisions include grades, school record, and test scores, followed by school counselor and teacher recommendations (The College Board, n.d.). The school counselor's honest opinion of a student's potential success in college can play a critical role; therefore, letters of recommendation are an opportunity to let the admissions committee see students with disabilities from a strengths-based perspective (see Table 6.4).

However, this is probably the most difficult aspect of the college admissions process for school counselors. If the student has decided to not disclose

Table 6.4 **Guidelines for Writing Letters of Recommendation**

DO gather information before writing the letter
 	
   • student self-assessment
 	
   • two or more teachers
 	
   • parents/guardians
 	
   • coaches/advisors
 	
DO develop an outline to organize the facts into topics
 	
DO use adjectives that describe this student
 	
DO find a way to bring this student to life for the reader
 	
DO include anecdotal information
 	
DO use specific references
 	
DO provide an overview that includes
 	
   • academic
 	
   • extracurricular
 	
   • volunteer activities
 	
DO demonstrate how this student
 	
   • stands out based on strengths
 	
   • makes a contribution
 	
   • has thought out future plans
 	
DO discuss what is relevant if you have permission to disclose any disability
 	
DO conclude with a paragraph that summarizes your strength of endorsement
	DON'T make the letter longer than one page
	
	DON'T use generic letters of recommendation
	
	DON'T agree to write a letter with one day's notice
	
	DON'T report grades because these are on the transcript
	
	DON'T disclose the disability unless you have permission to do so

his or her disability during the application process, the school counselor needs to be mindful of both the ethical and legal responsibilities in writing letters of recommendation. Federal law prohibits school counselors from divulging special education information about the student without parental permission—or that of the student, if he or she is of age (Family Educational Rights and Privacy Act, FERPA, 34 CFR Part 99; see Chapter 8). There is a fine line: "Legally, school counselors can include anything in a letter that is common knowledge and observable" (Stone, 2004, ¶4). However, ethically, it is still best practice to have the student's consent when including sensitive information. If, in your judgment, it is important to include sensitive information, be sure to secure student and parent permission. Because school counselors are strong student advocates, there is always a way to focus attention on a student's assets. In preparing letters of recommendation, gather information from a variety of sources, write clearly and concisely, focus on the student's strengths, and address the student's "fit" for the college.

Based on information provided by the College Board, the following suggested outline is a helpful guide for writing letters of recommendation:

¶1   Introduce the student; identify your relationship to the student and for what length of time; introduce main themes.

¶2   Focus on the student's academic strengths and areas for growth, performance related to ability; include anecdotal evidence and/or quotes to support your statements.

¶3   Areas of participation, distinctions; observations, comments, anecdotes to support your statements.

¶4   Personalize the recommendation; why you think this college is a good fit for this student.

¶5   Summary with a focus on impact this student has had in the school community, restatement of main themes, estimate of future performance, overall strength of endorsement.

Summary

School counselors play an important role in the collaborative team approach to address the challenges students with disabilities face as they navigate the various transitions during their school years. Providing support begins with the transition into kindergarten and continues through the transition into post-secondary options. School counselors can connect with students, parents, and other school personnel to have a planned program of responsive services. It is important that communication, information, and facilitation is from the perspective that "we are working together" to help all students experience positive transitions both vertically (e.g., grade to grade, school to school) and horizontally (e.g., between classrooms).

For postsecondary transition, school counselors need to be knowledgeable about the support services provided at a variety of colleges and to share this information with students and their parents as part of the college search process. It is important to note that students who have been supported by an IEP during their high school program will find the need to develop appropriate skills to advocate for themselves in the higher education community.

School counselors need to stay informed regarding current legislation as well as school policy regarding the appropriate disclosure of a disability. Chapter 7 discusses civil rights legislation covering students and adults with disabilities (i.e., Section 504 of the Rehabilitation Act of 1973, Americans With Disabilities Act, and ADA Amendments Act).

Reflective Questions

- What types of services can school counselors provide to students with disabilities in their elementary and secondary school transitions?

- How does the school counselor support students with disabilities in postsecondary planning, including applying to colleges?

Elementary-to-Middle School Transition Meeting Form

Student _____   School Year_____

School Counselor_____   Case Manager_____

Identify supports that have been successful, instructional strategies that have been helpful, and student's learning preferences based on elementary school experiences.

Supports	Strategies	Preferences

Date_____

The Role of the School Counselor in Section 504 of the Americans With Disabilities Act

Understanding 504

Special Education Program

Role of School Counselor

- Identification and implementation of appropriate classroom accommodations
- Resource on ADA legislation, policy and procedures
- Participant in evaluation and eligibility process

- Collaborative consultation
- Advocacy
- Inclusion
- Transitions
- Accountability

- Resource for students, parents, and staff on Section 504
- Facilitate and coordinates Section 504 meetings
- Case management including review and monitoring of Section 504 Plans

A Shared Vision of Special Education and School Counseling

Not all public school students with disabilities require special education instruction, and not all students meet the criteria for receiving special education support under the Individuals With Education Act (IDEA, 2006). Some students with disabilities may be eligible for classroom accommodations and support under a Civil Rights law, the Americans With Disabilities Act of 1990 (ADA). This law—and its update under the ADA Amendments Act of 2008, which also applies to Section 504 of the Rehabilitation Act of 1973—ensures that students with disabilities will receive equal access and eliminates discrimination in all school programs. What exactly is Section 504, and how does it impact the professional responsibilities of school counselors?

Section 504, IDEA, ADAAA, and the Definition of Disability

Both the Rehabilitation Act of 1973 and ADA are federal civil rights laws that protect individuals with disabilities and prohibit discrimination on the basis of disabling conditions in any program or activity that receives federal financial assistance. This includes all programs or activities of a school division, regardless of whether a specific program or activity directly receives or benefits from federal funds. Section 504 of the Rehabilitation Act of 1973 prohibited discrimination in access to employment, government (including its public schools, colleges, and universities), and public accommodations. The impact of Section 504 in schools is related to employment practices; program accessibility; and preschool, elementary, and secondary education.

Section 504 is enforced by the federal Office of Civil Rights (OCR). In its directives regarding meeting Section 504 requirements, OCR described an inclusive and least restrictive environment education setting for students with disabilities, consisting of "education in regular classrooms, education in regular classes with supplementary services, and/or special education and related services" (OCR, 2010, #4). Students may not be denied

IDEA Eligibility Criteria

To receive special education support under IDEA, students must meet the eligibility criteria in one of 13 federally recognized categories: autism, deaf-blindness, deafness, emotional disabilities, hearing impairment, intellectual disabilities, multiple disabilities, orthopedic impairment, other health impaired, specific learning disability, speech or language impairment, traumatic brain injury, and visual impairment (IDEA Regulations, 2006, 34 CFR ¶ 300.7). They must also require special education instruction.

participation in or benefit from services that are offered to their peers. Schools must ensure "handicapped persons equal opportunity to obtain the same result, to gain the same benefit, or to reach the same level of achievement, in the most integrated setting appropriate to the person's needs" (34 CFR Part 104).

Both Section 504 and IDEA guarantee that students and staff members will not be discriminated against by school districts. Because Section 504 is a civil rights act, the most important component is that students must have opportunities to access all activities and programs and cannot be denied participation because of their disability. Students who meet the definition of disability under IDEA are also protected under Section 504, but not all individuals who are protected from discrimination and provided accommodations under Section 504 qualify for protection and services under IDEA (see Figure

Figure 7.1 Student Population

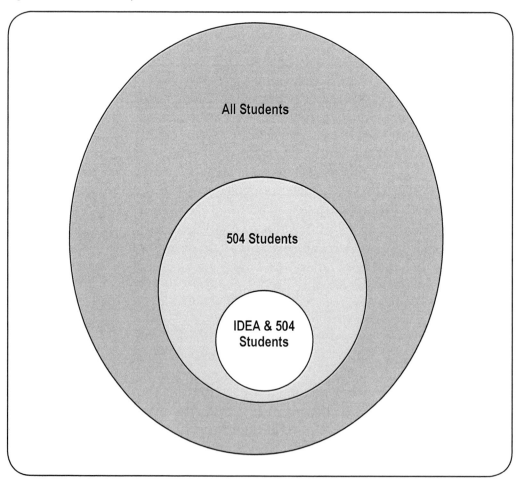

7.1). Table 7.1 provides a comparison of the differences between IDEA and Section 504, as they apply to public education.

Under Section 504, "disability means, with respect to an individual, a physical or mental impairment that substantially limits one or more of the major life activities of such individual; a record of such an impairment; or being regarded as having such an impairment (28 CFR § 36.104[3][iii]). The ADAAA, which included a "conforming amendment" to Section 504, (a) broadened the definition of disability, (b) increased the list of acceptable (but not exhaustive) "major life activities," and (c) limited the determination of whether an impairment substantially limits a major life activity based on mitigating measures. Learning, thinking, reading, and concentrating are all considered "major life activities" as a result of ADAAA.

The Role of the School Counselor in Section 504

As noted in Chapter 1, as legal and regulatory requirements have changed and the needs of students have increased, the role of the school counselor has continued to evolve. As Zirkel (2009) noted, "Section 504 is primarily the responsibility of teachers and administrators in general education" (p. 69). Madaus & Shaw (2008) examined the specific roles of school-based professionals to determine who oversaw the duties of coordinating Section 504 accommodations. At the school level, the duties of overseeing Section 504 fell to the principal or assistant principal (40%), followed by school counselors (21%), and school psychologists (15%). In reporting a follow-up survey, Madaus and Shaw (2008) noted that in "the individual schools reported in this study, general education administrators (e.g., principal, assistant principal) were followed by school counselors, school psychologists . . . in coordinating Section 504 meetings" (p. 375). Similarly, the study noted that Section 504 plans are "primarily managed by counselors, general education teachers, and school psychologists" (Madaus & Shaw, 2008, p. 375).

In many schools, the school counselor becomes the source of information for students, parents, and staff about Section 504; participates in the evaluation and eligibility procedures; facilitates Section 504 meetings; and acts as a case manager for 504 eligible students (see Figure 7.2). This role has both legal and ethical implications and requires that counselors add this information to their body of knowledge about students with disabilities. School counselors are involved in all aspects of student life, and therefore, should be well-informed of the differences between the IDEA and the ADA, and understand the intricacies surrounding each law.

Table 7.1   Comparison of IDEA and Section 504 in Public Education

Category	Special Education Law (IDEA)	Section 504 (as amended by ADAAA)
Purpose	Provides a free and appropriate public education to children and youth with specific disabilities	Prohibits discrimination on the basis of a person's disability in all programs receiving federal funds; provides a free and appropriate public education to children and youth with specific disabilities provides equal access to programs, services, and activities available to students without disabilities.
Eligibility	Evaluation for disability Must have need for special education	Evaluation for disability May not need special education
Age	Individuals 3–21	No age restriction
Disability	13 discrete categories of disabilities according to federal regulations	Any person who has a physical or mental impairment that substantially limits one or more major life activities, has a record of such an impairment, or is regarded as having such an impairment.
Referral	Child Find committee annually identifies and locates all children with disabilities who are not served	Committee of knowledgeable persons undertakes to identify and locate every qualified handicapped persons
Initial evaluation	Requires parental consent	Requires parental consent
Evaluation	Qualified professionals Multiple measures (including norm- and criterion-referenced tests) Prior written notice Tests administered in native language Input from parents	Trained evaluators Multiple measures to evaluate area of suspected need Prior written notice not required No guidance on administering tests in native language Input from parents not required
Procedural safeguards and due process rights	Notice of procedural safeguards Impartial Hearing Prior written notice Informed consent Access to educational records	Notice regarding evaluation or change in educational placement Impartial Hearing Prior written notice not required Informed consent not required but recognized as best practice Access to educational records

Table 7.1   Comparison of IDEA and Section 504 in Public Education (cont'd)

Category	Special Education Law (IDEA)	Section 504 (as amended by ADAAA)
FAPE	Special and general education and related services and aids	Special and general education and related services and aids
Educational Plan	IEP with mandated components that are reasonably calculated to convey educational benefit	Section 504 accommodation plan; no mandated components

Designed to meet the needs of students with disabilities as adequately as the needs of students without disabilities |
Related services	If required	If needed
Reevaluation	Every 3 years unless waived	Conducted on a periodic basis; reevaluation required prior to change in placement
Team	IEP team	Knowledgeable committee
Placement	Continuum of placement options in LRE	Continuum of placement options in LRE
Allows IEE	Yes, at district expense if parents disagree with district evaluation and district agrees to pay. But a district can challenge this request by filing due process and proving its elauation is appropriate	No
Discipline	10 consecutive school-day suspension limit without IDEA protections

Long-term removal if behavior not a manifestation of disability | 10 consecutive school-day suspension limit without IDEA protections

Long-term removal if behavior not a manifestation of disability |
Federal administering agency	U.S. Department of Education, Office of Special Education Programs	Office for Civil Rights, U.S. Department of Education
Compliance	State and local special education office	Compliance officer designated by the school division
Funding	Federal IDEA funds allocated for costs of educating children with disabilities	Not a funding statute
Responsibility	State and local special education agencies	Local general education agency

Note: IDEA = Individuals With Disabilities Education Act; ADAAA = Americans With Disabilities Act Amendments Act; FAPE = free appropriate public education; IEP = individualized education program; LRE = least restrictive environment; IEE = independent educational evaluation.

Figure 7.2 The School Counselor's Role in the Section 504 Process

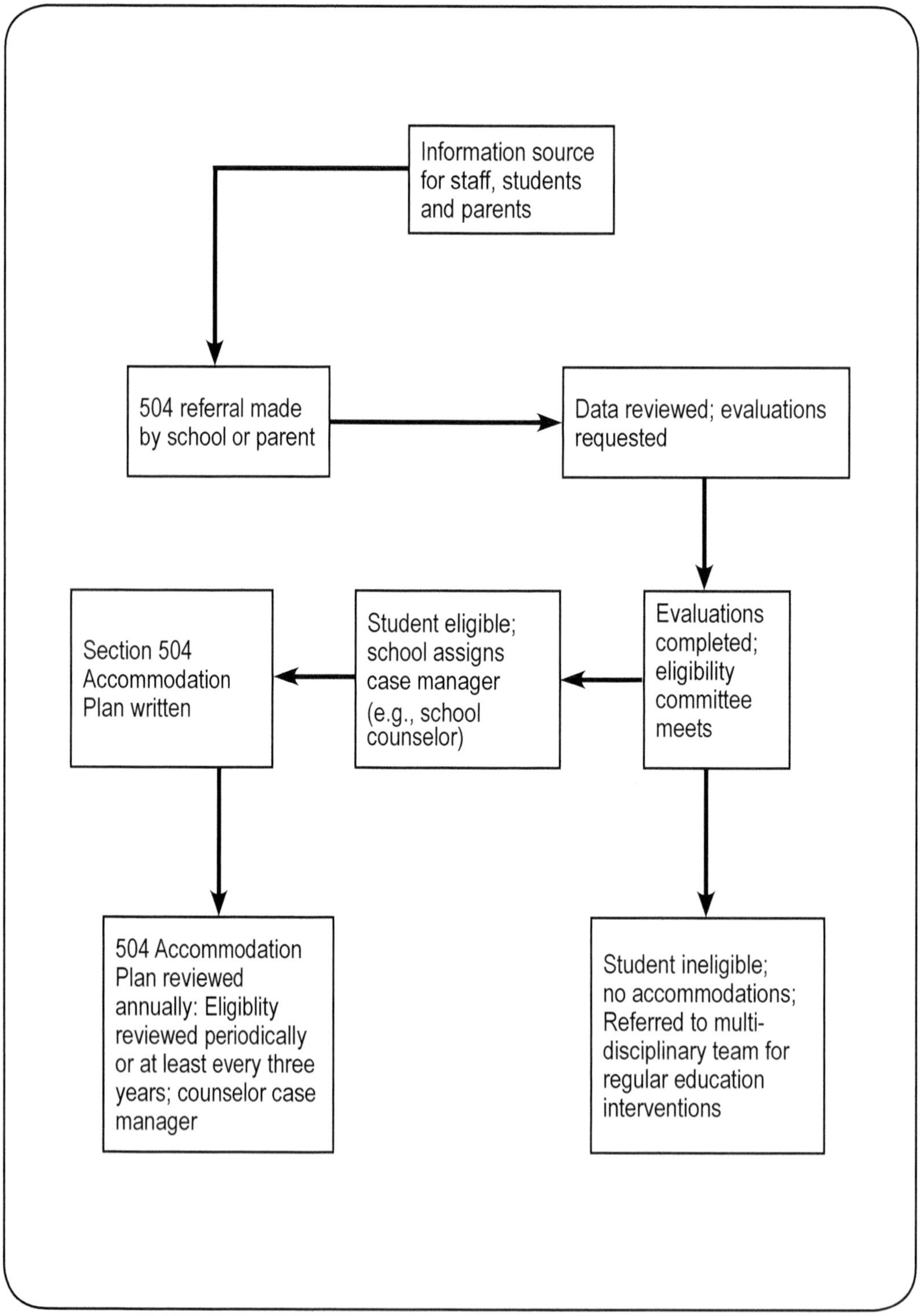

Information source
for staff, students
and parents

504 referral made
by school or parent

Data reviewed; evaluations
requested

Section 504
Accommodation
Plan written

Student eligible;
school assigns
case manager
(e.g., school
counselor)

Evaluations
completed;
eligibility
committee
meets

504 Accommodation
Plan reviewed
annually: Eligiblity
reviewed periodically
or at least every three
years; counselor case
manager

Student ineligible;
no accommodations;
Referred to multi-
disciplinary team for
regular education
interventions

The ADAAA/Section 504 Definition of Disability

In amending ADA, Congress was reacting to the Supreme Court and the Equal Employment Opportunity Commission's "too high a level of limitation in their interpretations of disability" (Benfer, 2009, p. 2). ADAAA expanded the list of qualifying impairments, and allowed more functions to be included under "major life activities," thus expanding and broadening the disability types that are protected. It should be noted that Congress also made clear that the definitions of *qualifying impairments* and *major life activities* were not all-inclusive, "and an activity not listed may be covered" (National Center for Learning Disabilities, 2009, p. 3). Table 7.2 delineates the differences between ADA and ADAAA definitions of disability.

Basically, under Section 504, a student is a student with a disability if he or she is (a) unable to perform a major life activity that the average student of approximately the same age can perform or (b) is significantly restricted as to the condition, manner, or duration under which a particular life activity is performed as compared to the average student of approximately the same age (29 C.F.R. § 1630.2[j]). Students with disabilities are expected to gain the same educational benefit as their peers, within the most integrated setting appropriate, but are not expected to produce identical results or the same level of achievement. Congress did not change the term "substantially limits" but established that the term was to be interpreted more broadly than "significantly restricted," which seemed "inconsistent with congressional intent, by expressing too high a standard" (Benfer, 2009, p.5). With ADAAA, Congress thus "achieved the goal of creating a lower standard" (Benfer, 2009, p. 2) for meeting the definition of disability.

ADAAA also stressed that an impairment substantially limiting one major life activity need not limit other major life activities in order to be considered a disability. For example, a student can be considered to have a disability if the impairment substantially limits, for example, reading, even if it does not limit learning. Under the

Mitigating Measures

Mitigating measures under ADAAA include, but are not limited to:

+ Medication

+ Medical equipment and supplies

+ Prosthetics including limbs and devices

+ Hearing aids and cochlear implants and other implantable hearing devices

+ Oxygen therapy equipment and supplies

+ Mobility devices

+ Low vision devices

+ Learned behavioral or adaptive neurological modification

+ Assistive technology or accommodations

+ Auxiliary aids or services

Table 7.2   Changes in ADA Definitions of Disability

Definition of a Disability Under ADA 1990	Definition of a Disability Under ADAAA of 2008
A physical or mental impairment is defined as any physiological disorder or condition, cosmetic disfigurement, or anatomical loss affecting one or more of the following body systems: neurological; musculoskeletal; special sense organs; respiratory, including speech organs; cardiovascular; reproductive; digestive; genitourinary; hemic and lymphatic; skin; and endocrine; or any mental or psychological disorder, such as mental retardation, organic brain syndrome, emotional or mental illness, and specific learning disabilities. This regulation does not list an exhaustive list of specific diseases and conditions because the list may not be comprehensive. [34 Code of Federal Regulations 104.3(j)(2)(i)].	A physical or mental impairment is defined as any physiological disorder or condition, cosmetic disfigurement, or anatomical loss affecting one or more of the following body systems: neurological; musculoskeletal; special sense organs; respiratory, including speech organs; cardiovascular; reproductive; digestive; genitourinary; hemic and lymphatic; skin; and endocrine; or any mental or psychological disorder, such as mental retardation, organic brain syndrome, emotional or mental illness, and specific learning disabilities. This regulation does not list an exhaustive list of specific diseases and conditions because the list may not be comprehensive. [34 Code of Federal Regulations 104.3(j)(2)(i)]. ADAAA ADDITIONS: Caring for one's self and performing manual tasks including: Seeing, hearing, eating, sleeping, walking, standing, lifting, bending, speaking, breathing, learning, reading, concentrating, thinking, communicating and working. The operation of a major bodily function (functions of the immune system, normal cell growth, digestive, bowel, bladder, neurological, brain, respiratory, circulatory, endocrine, and reproductive functions)

previous definition, the student would have had difficulty being found eligible if the impairment (in this case, reading) only affected one major life activity.

Mitigating Measures

ADAAA directs that schools must not consider the ameliorating effects of mitigating measures or use of auxiliary aids in considering whether an individual has a disability: The determination for eligibility is to be made without regard to mitigating measures, meaning that students may have a disability even if their condition is controlled by medication or physical aids. As an example, if a student with an attention deficit hyperactivity disorder takes medication to help him concentrate and focus in the classroom, the use of medication cannot be figured into the determination of whether or not the student has an impairment that substantially limits a major life activity.

Temporary vs. Episodic vs. History of Impairment

Another change to the determination of whether an impairment "substantially limits a major life activity" is that the decision must not be based on an impairment that is episodic or in remission if the impairment would substantially limit a major life activity if the episode was occurring, is active, or the illness is in full force. In other words, if a student has cancer that is in remission, that fact is not to be considered in the determination for Section 504.

The Office for Civil Rights (OCR) has, however, made it clear that a "temporary impairment" is not a disability under Section 504 unless the impairment results in a substantial limitation of one or more major life activities "for an extended period of time" (OCR, 2010). A student is not considered disabled if the impairment is transitory or minor with the actual expected duration of 6 months or less.

In addition, ADAAA expanded protection of individuals with a history of a disability. For example, a fourth-grade student who had leukemia as a child but since entering school has been in full remission should not be prevented from participating in any school programs or activities simply because of a history of an impairment. A student who, as a child, had a disease (e.g., tuberculosis) also cannot continue to be perceived as still having the disability or being treated in a discriminatory manner. These finer points most often relate to the areas of employment and postsecondary education; by themselves they are not sufficient to trigger Section 504 eligibility. Remember: To be eligible, the student's impairment needs to limit a major life activity.

Table 7.3   ADAAA and Student 504 Eligibility

Changes in the definition of impairment	Which major life activities are affected?	Mitigating measure (Cannot consider)	Remission or episodic?	Explanation for 504 Eligibility
Example 1: 4th-grade student has difficulty in reading but does not have a SLD	Reading	Private tutor 4x/week; extra help from reading teacher ⊘	N/A	Would be found eligible with an impairment in reading even though student receives extra reading support at school and home
Example 2: 1st-grade student has diabetes	Eating	Student goes to clinic daily to check blood sugar; takes insulin daily through pump ⊘	N/A	Student is eligible because he is limited in the endocrine function which necessitates insulin
Example 3: 7th-grade student has cancer and has not attended school for 3 weeks while a new medical protocol was tried.	Learning Eating Sleeping	Health plan in school; home-bound tutor provided by school division ⊘	Episodic	Student would be found eligible based on an impairment in normal cell growth function
Example 4: 3rd-grade student becomes depressed when her military mother is deployed	Caring for one's self Sleeping	School counselor meets with student informally; student take antidepressant medication ⊘	Episodic: occurs when parent leaves country	Student is eligible under inability to care for self and impact on sleeping
Example 5: 9th-grade student with severe asthma	Breathing	School has written health plan; student has inhaler ⊘	Episodic based on weather	Student is eligible under inability to breath, even though asthma is related only to spring allergies
Example 6: 12th-grade student is diagnosed with ADHD; he is in honors classes and receives grades of As and Bs	Concentrating	Student has 3–4 hours of homework nightly; takes medication for ADHD ⊘	NA	Student is eligible because learning is affected by the length of time it takes him to complete his homework, in comparison to his peers who only require half the time

Note. SLD = specific learning disability; ADHD = attention deficity hyperactivity disorder.

The intricate definition of a physical or mental impairment impacts the implementation of Section 504 for school counselors and school staff. ADAAA broadened the definition, added mitigating measures, and addressed duration of the impairment. In doing so, ADAAA made the application of the definition more extensive, and the effect of eligibility decisions far-reaching. Table 7.3 provides examples of the impact of the law in different areas of student eligibility.

Clearly, the passage of ADAAA has had a significant impact on Section 504 eligibility for students. An understanding of the nuances of the law is vital for school counselors, especially because ADAAA makes the law more complicated. Knowledge of the legal requirements of Section 504 is a "must-have" for school counselors. Counselors may be involved in student observations and reports, both verbal and written, and participate in the Section 504 eligibility committee. If assigned as case managers, they ensure that appropriate accommodations allowed under Section 504 are implemented.

The Process for Section 504 Services

Child Find and Referral Process

School divisions must have a Child Find and referral process that guarantees the school division will identify and locate qualified persons with a disability not receiving a free appropriate public education. The process for Section 504 is similar to the IDEA eligibility process (see Chapter 4). Timelines for Section 504 are based loosely on IDEA timelines. School districts establish procedures for evaluation of students suspected of needing special education because of a disability or impairment.

Section 504 referrals are considered when a parent requests an evaluation, if the school is considering suspension or expulsion, if a student exhibits an ongoing medical problem, and when a student transfers from

When to Consider a 504 Referral

- Parental request

- Suspension or expulsion is being considered

- Student is found ineligible for IDEA

- Student is found no longer eligible for IDEA

- Student has on-going medical issues or is chronically absent due to health issues

- Student receives medication at school

- Student performs academically lower than expected

- Student is found eligible for IDEA but parents refuse consent for services, or revoke consent for services after initial consent another school division or state with a current 504 plan. (See end of this chapter for a sample blank referral form.) Parental consent for Section 504 evaluations is required only for initial evaluation and placement. Even though not required, reevaluations are conducted periodically and in a reasonable amount of time. Best practice dictates following IDEA timelines.

Evaluations

"Section 504 requires the use of evaluation procedures that ensure that children are not misclassified, unnecessarily labeled as having a disability, or incorrectly placed, based on inappropriate selection, administration, or interpretation of evaluation materials" (OCR, 2010). Section 504 eligibility must consist of information from a variety of records and sources, such as:

- Teacher narratives, observations, attendance records, counselor reports, grades, report cards, high school transcripts, and discipline referrals;

- Informal classroom assessments such as curriculum based assessment (CBM), work samples, norm referenced educational assessments, and academic interventions;

- Physical condition and health information, medical diagnosis and evaluations, and doctor's notes;

- Social and cultural background and adaptive behavior;

- Information provided by parents or guardians (including private assessments).

Evaluation tools must be validated and provide more than a single intellectual quotient. Having a variety of materials ensures that the knowledgeable team receives a broad picture of the student to use in making eligibility decisions.

Eligibility

The eligibility committee should include persons knowledgeable about the student, the meaning of the data, and the placement options to be considered, within the context of the definition under Section 504: the nature of the physical or mental impairment(s); the nature and extent of the major life activities that are substantially limited by the impairment(s); and the impact of the substantial limitation of a major life activity on the student's opportunity to

Figure 7.3 Section 504 Eligibility

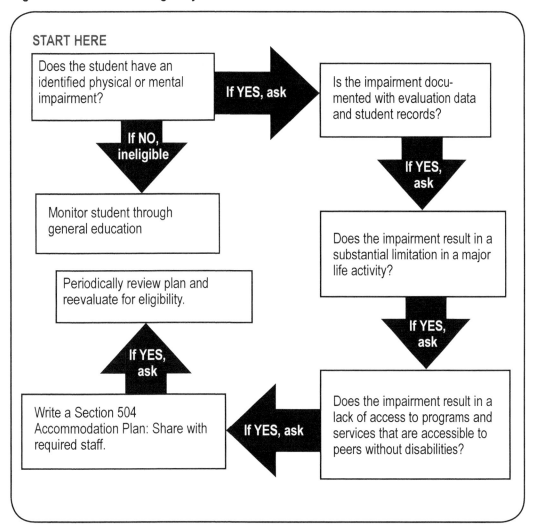

access programs and activities in the school setting (34 CFR § 104.35; see Figure 7.3).

Although information submitted by parents or guardians, including a medical diagnosis, must be considered by the committee, eligibility for Section 504 does not rest solely on private evaluations. The eligibility committee must consider private assessments, but there should be a clear correlation between the disability being considered and the limitation on the student. The school counselor, if chairing the eligibility committee, should follow district procedures while facilitating responsive dialogue among all members of the committee. (See end of this chapter for a sample eligibility form.)

Developing a Section 504 Plan

After a student has been found eligible under Section 504, the school needs to develop a plan for accommodating the student's disability (see sample, end of this chapter). The plan formalizes the accommodations, in writing, and is accomplished by a group of persons knowledgeable about the qualified student, including an administrator, school counselor, classroom teacher(s), specialists, and parent or guardian. The plan reflects the needs of the student for both classroom (academic) and extracurricular participation and is specifies accommodations that allow the student the opportunity to participate in or benefit from the school's programs and activities. Unlike an IEP, the Section 504 Plan does not contain goals and objectives or a present level of performance. It is not as expansive as an IEP, but is still a legal document that is to be precisely followed.

Best practice suggests that the committee should meet at least once a year to review the Section 504 Plan to ensure that the student's individual needs are being met. Following IDEA guidelines is a proactive way to ensure that Section 504 students receive appropriate accommodations that are reviewed at least as often as students eligible under IDEA. The committee should consider evaluation data relevant to the student's disability and ensures that the accommodations relate directly to the impairment.

Responsibilities of the Case Manager

It is the responsibility of the case manager to guarantee that (a) the accommodations in the plan are implemented, (b) the plan is periodically reviewed (approximately once a year), and (c) an eligibility review is conducted at least every 3 years. The case manager schedules meetings, facilitates the discussion, takes notes, and serves as the representative of the school district. The case manager (often, the school counselor) works closely with both the school staff and the parents to make certain the Section 504 Plan is correctly implemented.

Perhaps one of the most important aspects of a Section 504 Plan is ensuring that the accommodations that are written are appropriate for the student's impairment (see Table 7.4) and the committee participants understand and agree with the implementation of the accommodations. It is a delicate line between meeting the required components of ADA and Section 504, ensuring access to programs and activities, providing the student with the same benefit as his or her typically developing peers, and making sure that the accommodations are appropriate and reasonable. It is also important to inform all staff about a student's Section 504 Plan, including coaches and after-school staff. A student's rights under the ADAAA apply in nonacademic and extracurricular

Table 7.4   Possible Section 504 Plan Accommodations

Mental or Physical Impairment	Possible Accommodations
Mobility	Extra time to get to class
Colitis (bowel functions)	Use of bathroom whenever necessary
Learning	Written outline; extra texts
Concentrating	Extra time to complete tasks and assignments
Acid reflux (function of digestive system)	Access to clinic as needed
Diabetes (function of endocrine system)	Alternative snacks at specific time of day
Communicating	Printed directions/assistive technology
Hearing	Gain student's attention before giving directions; printed directions
Severe migraines (brain function)	Access to clinic as needed; extended time on assignments

activities as well as academic arenas, including field trips, after-school activities, child care, and athletic teams.

It is important to note that individual student needs should dictate the kind of accommodations in the Section 504 Plan. There should be a clear link between the impairment and the type of accommodation, and evaluation data and supporting documentation must clearly show that the student requires the accommodations to meet the educational needs in a manner that parallels students without disabilities. Accommodations for testing need to follow established guidelines.

Summary

The enactment of the Americans With Disability Amendment Act of 2008 will have a major impact on the number of students served, because the definitions of *thinking*, *concentrating*, and so on will be open to interpretation until OCR or the courts clarify the standards for school settings. Schools will most likely receive many more referrals for Section 504, and the number of students will increase—which will directly impact the role and responsibilities of the school counselor.

Comprehending Section 504 helps school counselors to explain to staff, students, and parents the legalities of a law whose intent is to ensure the provision of accessibility to programs and services available in public schools (see Table 7.5). As with all records, confidentiality for Section 504 students is required. Chapter 8 provides an overview and discussion of the rules of confidentiality and FERPA.

Reflective Questions

- Who is eligible for a Section 504 Plan?

- What are the legal requirements under Section 504?

Table 7.5   Understanding 504

Did You Do This?

1. Make a proper referral?

2. Provide parents with current information about Section 504?

3. Alert staff to the changes in the law?

4. Follow suggested time lines?

5. Work with the parents and staff to write a 504 accommodation plan?

6. Monitor students who are ill, absent, dealing with emotional issues?

7. Invite the general education teachers to participate in writing the 504 accommodation plan?

8. Assist the teaching staff in understanding the 504 accommodation plan is a legal document?

9. Determine eligibility without reference to mitigating measures?

10. Engage the parents in questions about the implications of the impairments at home?

Try not to say this:

Can the student do the homework with the assistance of medication or a tutor (otherwise mitigating measures)?

I'm sorry to hear that your child has asthma, but a health plan is sufficient to meet her needs.

Instead, say this:

How does your child's ADD impact his or her ability to do homework at night?

How does having asthma affect your child physically? Are there secondary issues?

Student:_____   DOB:_____

Grade:_____   School:_____

Parent/Guardian:_____   Phone(s):_____

Teacher:_____   Date:_____   .

Referred by:_____

A.   Reason for Referral

B.   History of Interventions

C.   Summary of Data Reviewed (health information, observations, class based assessments, teacher narratives, adaptive behavior testing scores, anecdotal reports)

D. Summary of Parent Information

E. Additional Information

Which major life activity(s) appears to be limited:

□ caring for self   □ eating   □ seeing

□ hearing   □ sleeping   □ breathing

□ standing   □ speaking   □ communicating

□ concentrating   □ perform manual tasks   □ walking

□ lifting   □ bending   □ learning

□ reading   □ thinking   □ immune system function

□ working   □ normal cell grow   □ digestive function

□ bladder function   □ neurological function   □ brain function

□ respiratory function   □ circulatory function   □ endocrine function

□ reproductive function □ other (please describe_____)

How is the major life activity(s) being limited?

Student:_____ DOB:_____

Grade:_____ School:_____

Parent/Guardian:_____ Phone(s):_____

Teacher:_____ Date:_____

After considering information from the following sources:

☐ Teacher observations   ☐ Testing data (state and district)

☐ Check lists   ☐ Achievement and standardized tests

☐ Medical information   ☐ Doctor recommendations

☐ Teacher narratives   ☐ Grades

☐ Previous evaluations   ☐ Attendance

The Section 504 Eligibility Committee has evaluated the student and determined (choose A or B):

A. The student DOES have a physical or mental disability that substantially limits one or more of the following major life activities:

☐ caring for self	☐ eating	☐ seeing
☐ hearing	☐ sleeping	☐ breathing
☐ standing	☐ speaking	☐ communicating
☐ concentrating	☐ perform manual tasks	☐ walking
☐ lifting	☐ bending	☐ learning
☐ immune system function	☐ reading	☐ thinking
☐ working	☐ normal cell grow	☐ digestive function
☐ bladder function	☐ neurological function	☐ brain function
☐ respiratory function	☐ circulatory function	☐ endocrine function
☐ reproductive function	☐ other (please describe_____)	

B. The student DOES NOT have a mental or physical disability that substantially limits one or more major life activities.

Justification for decision:

SECTION 504 ACCOMODATION PLAN

Student:_____   Date:_____

School:_____

Team Members' Signatures

      Name   Position   Knowledgeable About

Identified Disability and Major Life Activity

Necessary Accommodations and/or Related Services

Individual(s) Responsible for Implementation/Monitoring

Date Plan Begins _____

Date Plan Ends _____

FERPA
and Confidentiality

Ethical and Legal Practice
for School Counselors

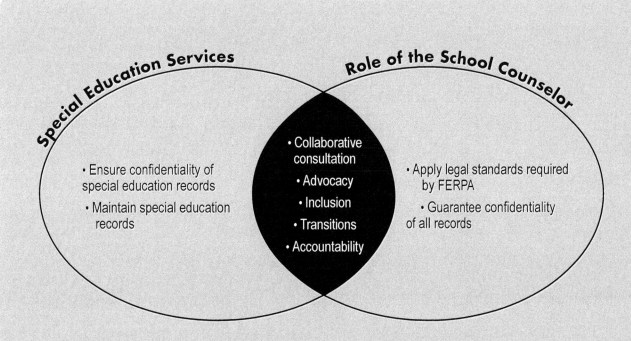

Special Education Services

Role of the School Counselor

- Ensure confidentiality of special education records
- Maintain special education records

- Collaborative consultation
- Advocacy
- Inclusion
- Transitions
- Accountability

- Apply legal standards required by FERPA
- Guarantee confidentiality of all records

A Shared Vision of Special Education and School Counseling

School counselors practice within the guidelines of professional ethical standards and the laws that have been established so that free and appropriate education is available for all students, regardless of disability. Chapter 2 discussed the *Ethical Standards for School Counselors* (American School Counselor Association, ASCA, 2010a; see Appendix B) with a specific focus on students with disabilities and special needs.

With increasing caseloads, decreasing school funds, and escalating responsibilities under the job description umbrella of "other duties as assigned," school counselors are hard-pressed to meet the demands of many masters. They must listen to parents advocating for more services or decrying that students are stigmatized with a disability label, or to those parents who have no idea what type of special education services should be provided to their children with disabilities. School counselors must respond to administrators who have fewer staff to provide the services legally required under the Individuals With Disabilities Education Act (IDEA, 2006), the American With Disabilities Act of 1990 (ADA), and the No Child Left Behind Act of 2001 (NCLB, 2006). Although many school counselors lack training in school law, it is important they stay informed about the legal implications for professional practice.

This chapter focuses on the Family Educational Rights and Privacy Act (FERPA) and confidentiality. Specific attention is given to the following: (a) protection of student privacy under FERPA, (b) when schools can disclose records without consent, (c) disclosure of information when shared by a minor in counseling, and (d) being a savvy user of technology.

Family Educational Rights and Privacy Act (FERPA)

Recent school tragedies involving students and teachers have brought to the forefront the need for school counselors to be informed of professional practice within FERPA guidelines. FERPA applies to all schools that receive funds from the U.S. Department of Education, and it protects the privacy of students' education records. FERPA gives certain rights to parents regarding their children's education records. These rights transfer to students when they reach the age of 18 or pursue their education beyond the high school level (i.e., "eligible students"). Parents and eligible students have the right to (a) inspect and review educational records, (b) seek correction if there are errors in the record, and (c) with some exceptions, obtain written permission of a parent before disclosing information contained in the student record (20 U.S.C. § 1232g). Generally, schools must have written permission from the parent or eligible student in order to release any information from a student's education record.

However, FERPA allows schools to disclose those records, without consent, to the following parties or under the following conditions:

- School officials with legitimate educational interest;

- Other schools to which a student is transferring;

- Specified officials for audit or evaluation purposes;

- Appropriate parties in connection with financial aid to a student;

- Organizations conducting certain studies for or on behalf of the school;

- Accrediting organizations;

- To comply with a judicial order or lawfully issued subpoena;

- Appropriate officials in cases of health and safety emergencies; and

- State and local authorities, within a juvenile justice system, pursuant to specific State law. (34 CFR § 99.31)

Further, schools may disclose without consent "directory information," such as a student's name, address, telephone number, date and place of birth, honors and awards, and dates of attendance (34 CFR § 99.31). However, parents and eligible students must be notified about the directory information and given a reasonable amount of time to request that the school not disclose the information. Parents and eligible students must be notified annually of their rights under FERPA. The means of notification is left to the discretion of the school and may be through a special letter, PTA or school bulletin, student handbook, or newspaper item.

Are E-Mails Educational Records?

Under FERPA, for an e-mail to qualify as an "educational record" it must personally identify the student and be maintained by the district. Documents that are placed in a student's permanent file are considered "maintained." If an e-mail is not in a student's permanent file, it is not considered an educational record. However, if an e-mail has been printed out and placed in the student's permanent file, it is considered an educational record.

Confidentiality

Confidentiality is covered in the ASCA *Ethical Standards for School Counselors* (2010a; see Appendix B) and pertains to the counseling relationship, handling, and disclosure of information that includes limits to confidentiality, student records, and personal data. The school counselor's primary obligation is to the student—balanced with "the legal and inherent rights of parents/guardians" (A.2.f.). Limits to confidentiality include (a) when there is clear and imminent danger to the student or others, (b) when legally required, (c) an identified third party whose relationship with the student may put him/her at high risk of contracting a communicable and fatal disease, (d) possible necessity of consulting with other professionals, (e) privileged communication, and (f) legal or authoritative restraints (A.2.a.).

Making decisions about whether there is "clear and imminent danger" to the student or others can be a slippery slope for school counselors. Therefore, school counselors need to know the state laws and school policies that guide their professional employment. Counselors should always consult with supervisors and colleagues on issues related to confidentiality.

As members of individualized education program (IEP) meetings, school counselors are expected to present information on a student's progress in counseling. However, they may not disclose specific details about individual counseling sessions. Two simple questions provide a basic guideline in determining what to share (Glossoff & Pate, 2002):

1. Do members of the team need to know this?

2. How will knowing this help the team make decisions to facilitate the student's educational progress?

Technology

School counselors have a variety of tools to assist in managing their workload, and many of these tools involve technology (e.g., computer programs, e-mail, voice mail, fax machines, cell phone, the Internet). With each of these forms of technology, there are ethical concerns that must be addressed, generally related to confidentiality. There is no guarantee of absolute confidentiality using any form of technology, so it is important for school counselors to enlist the highest level of privacy protocols. Standard practice procedures include using encryption software, passwords, and firewalls; enlisting the help of information technology professionals; following recommended guidelines for the safe use of technology; and attending workshops to increase skills and stay informed.

How many times have you heard about computer hackers and identity theft? Being vigilant when using a computer means not leaving information on the computer screen that may be viewed by others, not posting passwords in plain sight, and not leaving the computer unlocked when leaving the office. Instead, be a vigilant computer user who puts a privacy filter on the computer screen; positions the computer screen facing away from the office door; changes passwords on a frequent basis; uses passwords with a combination of upper and lower case letters, numerals, and symbols; stores passwords in a safe, secure place; sets the screen saver to appear when the computer has been idle; and "locks" the computer when stepping out of the office. With wise use, technology can save time, increase one's ability to professionally communicate with others, and provide an electronic trail of information (see Table 8.1).

Summary

FERPA exists to protect the privacy of student education records. The rights of parents and eligible students include inspecting and reviewing the education record, seeking corrections of errors in the education record, and ensuring written permission is obtained from the parent or eligible student before releasing information. Further, FERPA specifies when schools may disclose records without consent. It is important for school counselors to note that e-mail is not considered part of the education record unless it specifically identifies the student and has been printed out and placed in the student's permanent file.

Confidentiality is an important part of the school counselor's professional practice. Being able to determine what information is needed to be known and how the information can help make decisions in the best interests of the student are important guidelines to follow. Consulting with other professionals about decisions to share student information can provide school counselors with reassurance that they are using best practices both legally and ethically.

Technology can be a time saver and increase the school counselor's ability to access information and communicate with others. However, school counselors need to be mindful of the pitfalls and wisely use technology. Technology tips and e-mail etiquette included in this chapter are important guidelines for the savvy school counselor. (see Table 8.2)

Table 8.1   Technology Tips and E-mail Etiquette

Technology Tips	E-mail Etiquette
• Use anti-virus software.	• Be concise and to the point.
• Use a firewall.	• Use proper spelling, grammar, and punctuation.
• Keep your computer up to date with available security downloads.	• Be timely in replying to e-mails.
• Install anti-spyware.	• Try to avoid "fancy" fonts, colors, and formats.
• Change your passwords once a month.	• Develop templates you can use for frequently used responses.
• Never share passwords and don't post them in obvious places.	• Read your e-mail before you send it.
• Backup your e-mail on a regular basis.	• Take care when using abbreviations.
• Log out when you are not using your e-mail.	• Remember that when you type in CAPITALS it is indicating you are shouting.
• Make sure passwords contain letters, numbers, and symbols.	• Use a meaningful subject line.
• Lock your computer when you are away from it.	• Avoid using e-mail to discuss confidential information.
• Disconnect from the Internet when you are not using it.	• Use active rather than passive verbs.
• Review your settings to be sure your computer is adequately protected.	• Avoid long sentences.
• Protect your computer from power surges (i.e., electrical surge protectors).	• Avoid long e-mails.
• Backup your data frequently.	
• Watch out for spam and do not respond to "phishing" e-mails.	

Table 8.2   Understanding FERPA

Do You Do This?

1. Remember FERPA?

2. Protect the privacy of your students with disabilities?

3. Remember to keep confidential conversations private?

4. Alert the building administrator when inappropriate requests are made?

5. Keep confidential records in a safe place?

6. "Lock" your computer when you step out of the office?

7. Remember and observe e-mail etiquette?

Try not to say this:

> I would be happy to give you the names of a few of our special education students. They would be great for your newspaper article.

Instead, say this:

> The names of students with disabilities are confidential information, which is protected by IDEA and FERPA. You may contact someone in our communications office who can handle your request.

QUESTIONS   ANSWERS

Reflective Questions

- How does FERPA guide school counseling practice when it comes to disclosure of information?

- What do school counselors need to know about using technology to store and share information?

Appendix A

IDEA Definition of Disability Categories

Regulations: Part 300 / A / 300.8 / c

(c) Definitions of disability terms. The terms used in this definition of a child with a disability are defined as follows:

(1)

(i) Autism means a developmental disability significantly affecting verbal and nonverbal communication and social interaction, generally evident before age three, that adversely affects a child's educational performance. Other characteristics often associated with autism are engagement in repetitive activities and stereotyped movements, resistance to environmental change or change in daily routines, and unusual responses to sensory experiences.

(ii) Autism does not apply if a child's educational performance is adversely affected primarily because the child has an emotional disturbance, as defined in paragraph (c)(4) of this section.

(iii) A child who manifests the characteristics of autism after age three could be identified as having autism if the criteria in paragraph (c)(1)(i) of this section are satisfied.

(2) Deaf-blindness means concomitant hearing and visual impairments, the combination of which causes such severe communication and other developmental and educational needs that they cannot be accommodated in special education programs solely for children with deafness or children with blindness.

(3) Deafness means a hearing impairment that is so severe that the child is impaired in processing linguistic information through hearing, with or without amplification that adversely affects a child's educational performance.

(4)

(i) Emotional disturbance means a condition exhibiting one or more of the following characteristics over a long period of time and to a marked degree that adversely affects a child's educational performance:

(A) An inability to learn that cannot be explained by intellectual, sensory, or health factors.

(B) An inability to build or maintain satisfactory interpersonal relationships with peers and teachers.

(C) Inappropriate types of behavior or feelings under normal circumstances.

(D) A general pervasive mood of unhappiness or depression.

(E) A tendency to develop physical symptoms or fears associated with personal or school problems.

(ii) Emotional disturbance includes schizophrenia. The term does not apply to children who are socially maladjusted, unless it is determined that they have an emotional disturbance under paragraph (c)(4)(i) of this section.

(5) Hearing impairment means an impairment in hearing, whether permanent or fluctuating, that adversely affects a child's educational performance but that is not included under the definition of deafness in this section.

(6) Mental retardation means significantly subaverage general intellectual functioning, existing concurrently with deficits in adaptive behavior and manifested during the developmental period, that adversely affects a child's educational performance.

(7) Multiple disabilities means concomitant impairments (such as mental retardation-blindness or mental retardation-orthopedic impairment), the combination of which causes such severe educational needs that they cannot be accommodated in special education programs solely for one of the impairments. Multiple disabilities does not include deaf-blindness.

(8) Orthopedic impairment means a severe orthopedic impairment that adversely affects a child's educational performance. The term includes impairments caused by a congenital anomaly, impairments caused by disease (e.g., poliomyelitis, bone tuberculosis), and impairments from other causes (e.g., cerebral palsy, amputations, and fractures or burns that cause contractures).

(9) Other health impairment means having limited strength, vitality, or alertness, including a heightened alertness to environmental stimuli, that results in limited alertness with respect to the educational environment, that--

(i) Is due to chronic or acute health problems such as asthma, attention deficit disorder or attention deficit hyperactivity disorder, diabetes, epilepsy, a heart condition, hemophilia, lead poisoning, leukemia, nephritis, rheumatic fever, sickle cell anemia, and Tourette syndrome; and

(ii) Adversely affects a child's educational performance.

(10) Specific learning disability. (i) General. Specific learning disability means a disorder in one or more of the basic psychological processes involved in understanding or in using language, spoken or written, that may manifest itself in the imperfect ability to listen, think, speak, read, write, spell, or to do mathematical calculations, including conditions such as perceptual disabilities, brain injury, minimal brain dysfunction, dyslexia, and developmental aphasia.

> (ii) Disorders not included. Specific learning disability does not include learning problems that are primarily the result of visual, hearing, or motor disabilities, of mental retardation, of emotional disturbance, or of environmental, cultural, or economic disadvantage.

(11) Speech or language impairment means a communication disorder, such as stuttering, impaired articulation, a language impairment, or a voice impairment, that adversely affects a child's educational performance.

(12) Traumatic brain injury means an acquired injury to the brain caused by an external physical force, resulting in total or partial functional disability or psychosocial impairment, or both, that adversely affects a child's educational performance. Traumatic brain injury applies to open or closed head injuries resulting in impairments in one or more areas, such as cognition; language; memory; attention; reasoning; abstract thinking; judgment; problem-solving; sensory, perceptual, and motor abilities; psychosocial behavior; physical functions; information processing; and speech. Traumatic brain injury does not apply to brain injuries that are congenital or degenerative, or to brain injuries induced by birth trauma.

(13) Visual impairment including blindness means an impairment in vision that, even with correction, adversely affects a child's educational performance. The term includes both partial sight and blindness.

Appendix B

Ethical Standards for School Counselors

Ethical Standards for School Counselors

(Adopted 1984; revised 1992, 1998, 2004 and 2010)

Preamble

The American School Counselor Association (ASCA) is a professional organization whose members are school counselors certified/licensed in school counseling with unique qualifications and skills to address all students' academic, personal/social and career development needs. Members are also school counseling program directors/supervisors and counselor educators. These ethical standards are the ethical responsibility of school counselors. School counseling program directors/supervisors should know them and provide support for practitioners to uphold them. School counselor educators should know them, teach them to their students and provide support for school counseling candidates to uphold them.

Professional school counselors are advocates, leaders, collaborators and consultants who create opportunities for equity in access and success in educational opportunities by connecting their programs to the mission of schools and subscribing to the following tenets of professional responsibility:

- Each person has the right to be respected, be treated with dignity and have access to a comprehensive school counseling program that advocates for and affirms all students from diverse populations including: ethnic/racial identity, age, economic status, abilities/ disabilities, language, immigration status, sexual orientation, gender, gender identity/ expression, family type, religious/spiritual identity and appearance.

- Each person has the right to receive the information and support needed to move toward self-direction and self-development and affirmation within one's group identities, with special care being given to students who have historically not received adequate educational services, e.g., students of color, students living at a low socio-economic status, students with disabilities and students from non-dominant language backgrounds.

- Each person has the right to understand the full magnitude and meaning of his/her educational choices and how those choices will affect future opportunities.

- Each person has the right to privacy and thereby the right to expect the school-counselor/student relationship to comply with all laws, policies and ethical standards pertaining to confidentiality in the school setting.

- Each person has the right to feel safe in school environments that school counselors help create, free from abuse, bullying, neglect, harassment or other forms of violence. In this document, ASCA specifies the principles of ethical behavior necessary to maintain the high standards of integrity, leadership and professionalism among its members. The Ethical Standards for School Counselors were developed to clarify the nature of ethical responsibilities held in common by school counselors, supervisors/ directors of school counseling programs and school counselor educators. The purposes of this document are to: (Adopted 1984; revised 1992, 1998, 2004 and 2010)

- Serve as a guide for the ethical practices of all professional school counselors, supervisors/directors of school counseling programs and school counselor educators regardless of level, area, population served or membership in this professional association;

- Provide self-appraisal and peer evaluations regarding school counselors' responsibilities to students, parents/guardians, colleagues and professional associates, schools, communities and the counseling profession; and

- Inform all stakeholders, including students, parents and guardians, teachers, administrators, community members and courts of justice, of best ethical practices, values and expected behaviors of the school counseling professional.

A.1. Responsibilities to Students

Professional school counselors:

a. Have a primary obligation to the students, who are to be treated with dignity and respect as unique individuals.

b. Are concerned with the educational, academic, career, personal and social needs and encourage the maximum development of every student.

c. Respect students' values, beliefs and cultural background and do not impose the school counselor's personal values on students or their families.

d. Are knowledgeable of laws, regulations and policies relating to students and strive to protect and inform students regarding their rights.

e. Promote the welfare of individual students and collaborate with them to develop an action plan for success.

f. Consider the involvement of support networks valued by the individual students.

g. Understand that professional distance with students is appropriate, and any sexual or romantic relationship with students whether illegal in the state of practice is considered a grievous breach of ethics and is prohibited regardless of a student's age.

h. Consider the potential for harm before entering into a relationship with former students or one of their family members.

A.2. Confidentiality

Professional school counselors:

a. Inform individual students of the purposes, goals, techniques and rules of procedure under which they may receive counseling. Disclosure includes the limits of confidentiality in a developmentally appropriate manner. Informed consent requires competence on the part of students to understand the limits of confidentiality and Ethical Standards for School Counselors therefore, can be difficult to obtain from students of a certain developmental level. Professionals are aware that even though every attempt is made to obtain informed consent it is not always possible and when needed will make counseling decisions on students' behalf.

b. Explain the limits of confidentiality in appropriate ways such as classroom guidance lessons, the student handbook, school counseling brochures, school Web site, verbal notice or other methods of student, school and community communication in addition to oral notification to individual students.

c. Recognize the complicated nature of confidentiality in schools and consider each case in context. Keep information confidential unless legal requirements demand that confidential information be revealed or a breach is required to prevent serious and foreseeable harm to the student. Serious and foreseeable harm is different for each minor in schools and is defined by students' developmental and chronological age, the setting, parental rights and the nature of the harm. School counselors consult with appropriate professionals when in doubt as to the validity of an exception.

d. Recognize their primary obligation for confidentiality is to the students but balance that obligation with an understanding of parents'/guardians' legal and inherent rights to be the guiding voice in their children's lives, especially in value-laden issues. Understand the need to balance students' ethical rights to make choices, their capacity to give consent or assent and parental or familial legal rights and responsibilities to protect these students and make decisions on their behalf.

e. Promote the autonomy and independence of students to the extent possible and use the most appropriate and least intrusive method of breach. The developmental age and the circumstances requiring the breach are considered and as appropriate students are engaged in a discussion about the method and timing of the breach.

f. In absence of state legislation expressly forbidding disclosure, consider the ethical responsibility to provide information to an identified third party who, by his/her relationship with the student, is at a high risk of contracting a disease that is commonly known to be communicable and fatal. Disclosure requires satisfaction of all of the following conditions:

- Student identifies partner or the partner is highly identifiable

- School counselor recommends the student notify partner and refrain from further high-risk behavior

- Student refuses

- School counselor informs the student of the intent to notify the partner

- School counselor seeks legal consultation from the school district's legal representative in writing as to the legalities of informing the partner

g. Request of the court that disclosure not be required when the release of confidential information may potentially harm a student or the counseling relationship.

h. Protect the confidentiality of students' records and release personal data in accordance with prescribed federal and state laws and school policies including the laws within the Family Education Rights and Privacy

Act (FERPA). Student information stored and transmitted electronically is treated with the same care as traditional student records. Recognize the vulnerability of confidentiality in electronic communications and only transmit sensitive information electronically in a way that is untraceable to students' identity. Critical information such as a student who has a history of suicidal ideation must be conveyed to the receiving school in a personal contact such as a phone call.

A.3. Academic, Career/College/Post-Secondary Access and Personal/Social Counseling Plans

Professional school counselors:

a. Provide students with a comprehensive school counseling program that parallels the ASCA National Model with emphasis on working jointly with all students to develop personal/social, academic and career goals.

b. Ensure equitable academic, career, post-secondary access and personal/ social opportunities for all students through the use of data to help close achievement gaps and opportunity gaps.

c. Provide and advocate for individual students' career awareness, exploration and post-secondary plans supporting the students' right to choose from the wide array of options when they leave secondary education.

A.4. Dual Relationships Professional school counselors:

a. Avoid dual relationships that might impair their objectivity and increase the risk of harm to students (e.g., counseling one's family members or the children of close friends or associates). If a dual relationship is unavoidable, the school counselor is responsible for taking action to eliminate or reduce the potential for harm to the student through use of safeguards, which might include informed consent, consultation, supervision and documentation.

b. Maintain appropriate professional distance with students at all times.

c. Avoid dual relationships with students through communication mediums such as social networking sites.

d. Avoid dual relationships with school personnel that might infringe on the integrity of the school counselor/student relationship.

A.5. Appropriate Referrals Professional school counselors:

a. Make referrals when necessary or appropriate to outside resources for student and/or family support. Appropriate referrals may necessitate informing both parents/guardians and students of applicable resources and making proper plans for transitions with minimal interruption of services. Students retain the right to discontinue the counseling relationship at any time.

b. Help educate about and prevent personal and social concerns for all students within the school counselor's scope of education and competence and make necessary referrals when the counseling needs are beyond the individual school counselor's education and training. Every attempt is made to find appropriate specialized resources for clinical therapeutic topics that are difficult or inappropriate to address in a school setting such as eating disorders, sexual trauma, chemical dependency and other addictions needing sustained clinical duration or assistance.

c. Request a release of information signed by the student and/or parents/guardians when attempting to develop a collaborative relationship with other service providers assigned to the student.

d. Develop a reasonable method of termination of counseling when it becomes apparent that counseling assistance is no longer needed or a referral is necessary to better meet the student's needs.

A.6. Group Work Professional school counselors:

a. Screen prospective group members and maintain an awareness of participants' needs, appropriate fit and personal goals in relation to the group's intention and focus. The school counselor takes reasonable precautions to protect members from physical and psychological harm resulting from interaction within the group.

b. Recognize that best practice is to notify the parents/guardians of children participating in small groups.

c. Establish clear expectations in the group setting, and clearly state that confidentiality in group counseling cannot be guaranteed. Given the developmental and chronological ages of minors in schools, recognize the tenuous nature of confidentiality for minors renders some topics inappropriate for group work in a school setting.

d. Provide necessary follow up with group members, and document proceedings as appropriate.

e. Develop professional competencies, and maintain appropriate education, training and supervision in group facilitation and any topics specific to the group.

f. Facilitate group work that is brief and solution-focused, working with a variety of academic, career, college and personal/social issues.

A.7. Danger to Self or Others Professional school counselors:

a. Inform parents/guardians and/or appropriate authorities when a student poses a danger to self or others. This is to be done after careful deliberation and consultation with other counseling professionals.

b. Report risk assessments to parents when they underscore the need to act on behalf of a child at risk; never negate a risk of harm as students sometimes deceive in order to avoid further scrutiny and/or parental notification.

c. Understand the legal and ethical liability for releasing a student who is in danger to self or others without proper and necessary support for that student.

A.8. Student Records Professional school counselors:

a. Maintain and secure records necessary for rendering professional services to the student as required by laws, regulations, institutional procedures and confidentiality guidelines.

b. Keep sole-possession records or individual student case notes separate from students' educational records in keeping with state laws.

c. Recognize the limits of sole-possession records and understand these records are a memory aid for the creator and in absence of privileged communication may be subpoenaed and may become educational records when they are shared or are accessible to others in either verbal or written form or when they include information other than professional opinion or personal observations.

d. Establish a reasonable timeline for purging sole-possession records or case notes. Suggested guidelines include shredding sole possession records when the student transitions to the next level, transfers to another school or graduates. Apply careful discretion and deliberation before destroying sole-possession records that may be needed by a court of law such as notes on child abuse, suicide, sexual harassment or violence.

e. Understand and abide by the Family Education Rights and Privacy Act (FERPA, 1974), which safeguards student's records and allows parents to have a voice in what and how information is shared with others regarding their child's educational records.

A.9. Evaluation, Assessment and Interpretation Professional school counselors:

a. Adhere to all professional standards regarding selecting, administering and interpreting assessment measures and only utilize assessment measures that are within the scope of practice for school counselors and for which they are trained and competent.

b. Consider confidentiality issues when utilizing evaluative or assessment instruments and electronically based programs.

c. Consider the developmental age, language skills and level of competence of the student taking the assessments before assessments are given.

d. Provide interpretation of the nature, purposes, results and potential impact of assessment/evaluation measures in language the students can understand.

e. Monitor the use of assessment results and interpretations, and take reasonable steps to prevent others from misusing the information.

f. Use caution when utilizing assessment techniques, making evaluations and interpreting the performance of populations not represented in the norm group on which an instrument is standardized.

g. Assess the effectiveness of their program in having an impact on students' academic, career and personal/social development through accountability measures especially examining efforts to close achievement, opportunity and attainment gaps.

A.10. Technology Professional school counselors:

a. Promote the benefits of and clarify the limitations of various appropriate technological applications. Professional school counselors promote technological applications (1) that are appropriate for students' individual needs, (2) that students understand how to use and (3) for which follow-up counseling assistance is provided.

b. Advocate for equal access to technology for all students, especially those historically underserved.

c. Take appropriate and reasonable measures for maintaining confidentiality of student information and educational records stored or transmitted through the use of computers, facsimile machines, telephones, voicemail, answering machines and other electronic or computer technology.

d. Understand the intent of FERPA and its impact on sharing electronic student records.

e. Consider the extent to which cyberbullying is interfering with students' educational process and base guidance curriculum and intervention programming for this pervasive and potentially dangerous problem on research-based and best practices.

A.11. Student Peer Support Program Professional school counselors:

a. Have unique responsibilities when working with peer-helper or student-assistance programs and safeguard the welfare of students participating in peer-to-peer programs under their direction.

b. Are ultimately responsible for appropriate training and supervision for students serving as peer-support individuals in their school counseling programs.

B. RESPONSIBILITIES TO PARENTS/GUARDIANS

B.1. Parent Rights and Responsibilities

Professional school counselors:

a. Respect the rights and responsibilities of parents/guardians for their children and endeavor to establish, as appropriate, a collaborative relationship with parents/guardians to facilitate students' maximum development.

b. Adhere to laws, local guidelines and ethical standards of practice when assisting parents/guardians experiencing family difficulties interfering with the student's effectiveness and welfare.

c. Are sensitive to diversity among families and recognize that all parents/guardians, custodial and noncustodial, are vested with certain rights and responsibilities for their children's welfare by virtue of their role and according to law.

d. Inform parents of the nature of counseling services provided in the school setting.

e. Adhere to the FERPA act regarding disclosure of student information.

f. Work to establish, as appropriate, collaborative relationships with parents/guardians to best serve student.

B.2. Parents/Guardians and Confidentiality

Professional school counselors:

a. Inform parents/guardians of the school counselor's role to include the confidential nature of the counseling relationship between the counselor and student.

b. Recognize that working with minors in a school setting requires school counselors to collaborate with students' parents/guardians to the extent possible.

c. Respect the confidentiality of parents/guardians to the extent that is reasonable to protect the best interest of the student being counseled.

d. Provide parents/guardians with accurate, comprehensive and relevant information in an objective and caring manner, as is appropriate and consistent with ethical responsibilities to the student.

e. Make reasonable efforts to honor the wishes of parents/guardians concerning information regarding the student unless a court order expressly forbids the involvement of a parent(s). In cases of divorce or separation, school counselors exercise a good-faith effort to keep both parents informed, maintaining focus on the student and avoiding supporting one parent over another in divorce proceedings.

C. RESPONSIBILITIES TO COLLEAGUES AND PROFESSIONAL ASSOCIATES

C.1. Professional Relationships

Professional school counselors, the school counseling program director/site supervisor and the school counselor educator:

a. Establish and maintain professional relationships with faculty, staff and administration to facilitate an optimum counseling program.

b. Treat colleagues with professional respect, courtesy and fairness.

c. Recognize that teachers, staff and administrators who are highfunctioning in the personal and social development skills can be powerful allies in supporting student success. School counselors work to develop relationships with all faculty and staff in order to advantage students.

d. Are aware of and utilize related professionals, organizations and other resources to whom the student may be referred.

C.2. Sharing Information with Other Professionals

Professional school counselors:

a. Promote awareness and adherence to appropriate guidelines regarding confidentiality, the distinction between public and private information and staff consultation.

b. Provide professional personnel with accurate, objective, concise and meaningful data necessary to adequately evaluate, counsel and assist the student.

c. Secure parental consent and develop clear agreements with other mental health professionals when a student is receiving services from another counselor or other mental health professional in order to avoid confusion and conflict for the student and parents/guardians.

d. Understand about the "release of information" process and parental rights in sharing information and attempt to establish a cooperative and collaborative relationship with other professionals to benefit students.

e. Recognize the powerful role of ally that faculty and administration who function high in personal/social development skills can play in supporting students in stress, and carefully filter confidential information to give these allies what they "need to know" in order to advantage the student. Consultation with other members of the school counseling profession is helpful in determining need-to-know information. The primary focus and obligation is always on the student when it comes to sharing confidential information.

f. Keep appropriate records regarding individual students, and develop a plan for transferring those records to another professional school counselor should the need occur. This documentation transfer will protect the confidentiality and benefit the needs of the student for whom the records are written.

C.3. Collaborating and Educating Around the Role of the School Counselor

The school counselor, school counseling program supervisor/director and school counselor educator:

a. Share the role of the school counseling program in ensuring data driven academic, career/college and personal/social success competencies for every student, resulting in specific outcomes/indicators with all stakeholders.

b. Broker services internal and external to the schools to help ensure every student receives the benefits of a school counseling program and specific academic, career/college and personal/social competencies.

D. RESPONSIBILITIES TO SCHOOL, COMMUNITIES AND FAMILIES

D.1. Responsibilities to the School

Professional school counselors:

a. Support and protect students' best interest against any infringement of their educational program.

b. Inform appropriate officials, in accordance with school policy, of conditions that may be potentially disruptive or damaging to the school's mission, personnel and property while honoring the confidentiality between the student and the school counselor.

c. Are knowledgeable and supportive of their school's mission, and connect their program to the school's mission.

d. Delineate and promote the school counselor's role, and function as a student advocate in meeting the needs of those served. School counselors will notify appropriate officials of systemic conditions that may limit or curtail their effectiveness in providing programs and services.

e. Accept employment only for positions for which they are qualified by education, training, supervised experience, state and national professional credentials and appropriate professional experience.

f. Advocate that administrators hire only qualified, appropriately trained and competent individuals for professional school counseling positions.

g. Assist in developing: (1) curricular and environmental conditions appropriate for the school and community; (2) educational procedures and programs to meet students' developmental needs; (3) a systematic evaluation process for comprehensive, developmental, standards-based school counseling programs, services and personnel; and (4) a data-driven evaluation process guiding the comprehensive, developmental school counseling program and service delivery.

D.2. Responsibility to the Community

Professional school counselors:

a. Collaborate with community agencies, organizations and individuals in students' best interest and without regard to personal reward or remuneration.

b. Extend their influence and opportunity to deliver a comprehensive school counseling program to all students by collaborating with community resources for student success.

c. Promote equity for all students through community resources.

d. Are careful not to use their professional role as a school counselor to benefit any type of private therapeutic or consultative practice in which they might be involved outside of the school setting.

E. RESPONSIBILITIES TO SELF

E.1. Professional Competence Professional school counselors:

a. Function within the boundaries of individual professional competence and accept responsibility for the consequences of their actions.

b. Monitor emotional and physical health and practice wellness to ensure optimal effectiveness. Seek physical or mental health referrals when needed to ensure competence at all times

c. Monitor personal responsibility and recognize the high standard of care a professional in this critical position of trust must maintain on and off the job and are cognizant of and refrain from activity that may lead to inadequate professional services or diminish their effectiveness with school community members Professional and personal growth are ongoing throughout the counselor's career. d. Strive through personal initiative to stay abreast of current research and to maintain professional competence in advocacy, teaming and collaboration, culturally competent counseling and school counseling program coordination, knowledge and use of technology, leadership, and equity assessment using data.

e. Ensure a variety of regular opportunities for participating in and facilitating professional development for self and other educators and school counselors through continuing education opportunities annually including: attendance at professional school counseling conferences; reading Professional School Counseling journal articles; facilitating workshops for education staff on issues school counselors are uniquely positioned to provide.

f. Enhance personal self-awareness, professional effectiveness and ethical practice by regularly attending presentations on ethical decision- making. Effective school counselors will seek supervision when ethical or professional questions arise in their practice.

g. Maintain current membership in professional associations to ensure ethical and best practices.

E.2. Multicultural and Social Justice Advocacy and Leadership

Professional school counselors:

a. Monitor and expand personal multicultural and social justice advocacy awareness, knowledge and skills. School counselors strive for exemplary cultural competence by ensuring personal beliefs or values are not imposed on students or other stakeholders.

b. Develop competencies in how prejudice, power and various forms of oppression, such as ableism, ageism, classism, familyism, genderism, heterosexism, immigrationism, linguicism, racism, religionism and sexism, affect self, students and all stakeholders.

c. Acquire educational, consultation and training experiences to improve awareness, knowledge, skills and effectiveness in working with diverse populations: ethnic/racial status, age, economic status, special needs, ESL or ELL, immigration status, sexual orientation, gender, gender identity/expression, family type, religious/spiritual identity and appearance.

d. Affirm the multiple cultural and linguistic identities of every student and all stakeholders. Advocate for equitable school and school counseling program policies and practices for every student and all stakeholders including use of translators and bilingual/ multilingual school counseling program materials that represent all languages used by families in the school community, and advocate for appropriate accommodations and accessibility for students with disabilities.

e. Use inclusive and culturally responsible language in all forms of communication.

f. Provide regular workshops and written/digital information to families to increase understanding, collaborative two-way communication and a welcoming school climate between families and the school to promote increased student achievement.

g. Work as advocates and leaders in the school to create equitybased school counseling programs that help close any achievement, opportunity and attainment gaps that deny all students the chance to pursue their educational goals.

F. RESPONSIBILITIES TO THE PROFESSION

F.1. Professionalism

Professional school counselors:

a. Accept the policies and procedures for handling ethical violations as a result of maintaining membership in the American School Counselor Association.

b. Conduct themselves in such a manner as to advance individual ethical practice and the profession.

c. Conduct appropriate research, and report findings in a manner consistent with acceptable educational and psychological research practices. School counselors advocate for the protection of individual students' identities when using data for research or program planning.

d. Seek institutional and parent/guardian consent before administering any research, and maintain security of research records.

e. Adhere to ethical standards of the profession, other official policy statements, such as ASCA's position statements, role statement and the ASCA National Model and relevant statutes established by federal, state and local governments, and when these are in conflict work responsibly for change. f. Clearly distinguish between statements and actions made as a private individual and those made as a representative of the school counseling profession.

g. Do not use their professional position to recruit or gain clients, consultees for their private practice or to seek and receive unjustified personal gains, unfair advantage, inappropriate relationships or unearned goods or services.

F.2. Contribution to the Profession

Professional school counselors:

a. Actively participate in professional associations and share results and best practices in assessing, implementing and annually evaluating the outcomes of data-driven school counseling programs with measurable academic, career/ college and personal/social competencies for every student.

b. Provide support, consultation and mentoring to novice professionals.

c. Have a responsibility to read and abide by the ASCA Ethical Standards and adhere to the applicable laws and regulations.

F.3 Supervision of School Counselor Candidates Pursuing Practicum and Internship Experiences:

Professional school counselors:

a. Provide support for appropriate experiences in academic, career, college access and personal/social counseling for school counseling interns.

b. Ensure school counselor candidates have experience in developing, implementing and evaluating a data-driven school counseling program model, such as the ASCA National Model.

c. Ensure the school counseling practicum and internship have specific, measurable service delivery, foundation, management and accountability systems.

d. Ensure school counselor candidates maintain appropriate liability insurance for the duration of the school counseling practicum and internship experiences.

e. Ensure a site visit is completed by a school counselor education faculty member for each practicum or internship student, preferably when both the school counselor trainee and site supervisor are present.

F.4 Collaboration and Education about School Counselors and School Counseling Programs with other Professionals

School counselors and school counseling program directors/supervisors collaborate with special educators, school nurses, school social workers, school psychologists, college counselors/ admissions officers, physical therapists, occupational therapists and speech pathologists to advocate for optimal services for students and all other stakeholders.

G. MAINTENANCE OF STANDARDS

Professional school counselors are expected to maintain ethical behavior at all times.

G.1. When there exists serious doubt as to the ethical behavior of a colleague(s) the following procedure may serve as a guide:

1. The school counselor should consult confidentially with a professional colleague to discuss the nature of a complaint to see if the professional colleague views the situation as an ethical violation.

2. When feasible, the school counselor should directly approach the colleague whose behavior is in question to discuss the complaint and seek resolution.

3. The school counselor should keep documentation of all the steps taken.

4. If resolution is not forthcoming at the personal level, the school counselor shall utilize the channels established within the school, school district, the state school counseling association and ASCA's Ethics Committee.

5. If the matter still remains unresolved, referral for review and appropriate action should be made to the Ethics Committees in the following sequence:

- State school counselor association

- American School Counselor Association

6. The ASCA Ethics Committee is responsible for:

- Educating and consulting with the membership regarding ethical standards

- Periodically reviewing and recommending changes in code

- Receiving and processing questions to clarify the application of such standards. Questions must be submitted in writing to the ASCA Ethics Committee chair.

- Handling complaints of alleged violations of the ASCA Ethical Standards for School Counselors. At the national level, complaints should be submitted in writing to the ASCA Ethics Committee, c/o the Executive Director, American School Counselor Association, 1101 King St., Suite 625, Alexandria, VA 22314.

G.2. When school counselors are forced to work in situations or abide by policies that do not reflect the ethics of the profession, the school counselor works responsibly through the correct channels to try and remedy the condition.

G.3. When faced with any ethical dilemma school counselors, school counseling program directors/supervisors and school counselor educators use an ethical decision-making model such as Solutions to Ethical Problems in Schools (STEPS) (Stone, 2001):

1. Define the problem emotionally and intellectually.

2. Apply the ASCA Ethical Standards and the law.

3. Consider the students' chronological and developmental levels.

4. Consider the setting, parental rights and minors' rights.

5. Apply the moral principles.

6. Determine Your potential courses of action and their consequences.

7. Evaluate the selected action.

8. Consult

9. Implement the course of action.

Glossary of Special Education Acronyms

ABA	Applied behavioral analysis
ADA	Americans With Disabilities Act
ADD/ADHD	Attention deficit disorder/attention deficit hyperactivity disorder
ASD	Autism spectrum disorder
ASL	American Sign Language
AT	Assistive technology
AYP	Adequate yearly progress
BD	Behavioral disorder
BICS	Basic interpersonal communication skills
BIP	Behavior intervention plan
CA	Chronological age
CALPS	Cognitive academic language proficiency skills
CEC	Council for Exceptional Children
CF	Cystic fibrosis
CFR	Code of federal regulations
CP	Cerebral palsy
CST	Child study team
DB	Deaf-blindness
DD	Developmental delay
DR	Dispute resolution
DSM	Diagnostic and Statistical Manual of Mental Disorders
EC	Early childhood
ECE	Early childhood education
ED	Emotional disability
ED	U.S. Department of Education
EIP	Early intervention program
ELL	English language learner
ESOL	English for speakers of other languages
ESY	Extended school year
FAPE	Free and appropriate public education
FAS	Fetal alcohol syndrome
FBA	Functional behavioral assessment
FC	Functional communication
FERPA	Family Educational Rights and Privacy Act
FOIA	Freedom of Information Act
GT	Gifted and talented

HI	Hearing impaired
HO	Hearing officer
IA	Instructional assistant
IAES	Interim alternative educational setting
ID	Intellectual disability
IDEA	Individuals With Disabilities Education Act
IEE	Independent educational evaluation
IEP	Individualized education program
IFSP	Individualized family service plan
IQ	Intelligence quotient
ITP	Individualized transition plan
LD	Learning disability
LEP	Limited English proficiency
LRE	Least restrictive environment
MD	Muscular dystrophy
MD	Multiple disabilities
MR	Mental retardation
NCLB	No Child Left Behind Act
OCD	Obsessive-compulsive disorder
OCR	Office for Civil Rights
ODD	Oppositional defiant disorder
OHI	Other health impairment
OI	Orthopedic impairment
OT	Occupational therapy
PBIS	Positive behavioral intervention and supports
PBS	Positive behavioral supports
PD	Physical disability
PDD	Pervasive developmental disorder
PDD-NOS	Pervasive developmental disorder-not otherwise specified
PLEP	Present level of educational performance or present level of performance
PT	Physical therapy
RTI	Response to intervention
SAS	Supplementary aids and services
SAT	Student assistance team
SE	Special education
SEAC	Special education advisory committee

Section 504	Section 504 of the Rehabilitation Act of 1973
SED	Serious emotional disturbance
SI	Sensory integration
SIT	Student intervention team
SLD	Specific learning disability
S/L I	Speech and language impairment
SSDI	Social Security disability income
SSI	Supplemental security income
SST	Student study team
SWD	Students with disabilities
TAT	Teacher assistance team
TBI	Traumatic brain injury
VI	Visual Impairment

References

ADA Amendments Act of 2008, P. L. 110-325, 122 Stat. 3553, to be codified at 42 U.S.C. § 12101 (2009).

ADAAA Regulations (Title III), 28 CFR § 36 (2009).

Akos, P. (2002). Student perceptions of the transition from elementary to middle school. *Professional School Counseling, 5*(5), 339–345.

Akos, P., & Galassi, J. P. (2004). Middle and high school transitions as viewed by students, parents, and teachers. *Professional School Counseling, 7,* 212–221.

American Recovery and Reinvestment Act of 2009, Pub. L. No. 111-5, 123 Stat. 115, to be codified at 26 U.S.C. § 1 (2009).

American School Counselor Association. (2005a). *The ASCA national model: A framework for school counseling programs* (2nd ed.). Alexandria, VA: Author.

American School Counselor Association. (2005b). *Position statement: The professional school counselor and comprehensive school counseling programs.* Alexandria, VA: Author.

American School Counselor Association. (2007). *Position statement: The professional school counselor and discipline.* Alexandria, VA: Author. Retrieved from http://asca2.timberlakepublishing.com//files/PS_Discipline.pdf

American School Counselor Association. (2009). *Position statement: The professional school counselor and credentialing and licensure.* Alexandria, VA: Author. Retrieved from http://asca2.timberlakepublishing.com//files/Credentialing.pdf

American School Counselor Association. (2010a). *Ethical standards for school counselors.* Alexandria, VA: Author.

American School Counselor Association. (2010b). *Position statement: The professional school counselor and students with special needs.* Alexandria, VA: Author. Retrieved from http://asca2.timberlakepublishing.com//files/SpecialNeeds.pdf

American School Counselor Association. (2010c). *Student/school counselor ratio by state 2008–2009.* Alexandria, VA: Author. Retrieved from http://www.schoolcounselor.org/files/ratios%202008-2009.pdf

Americans With Disabilities Act of 1990, 42 U.S.C. § 12101 *et seq.* (2006).

Anderson-Butcher, D., & Ashton, D. (2004). Innovative models of collaboration to serve children, youths, families, and communities. *Children & Schools, 26*, 39–53.

Augst, K., & Akos, P. (2009). Primary transitions: How elementary school counselors promote optimal transitions. *Journal of School Counseling, 7*, 1–34.

Baditoi, B. E. (2010). *When behavior makes learning hard: Positive steps for changing student behavior.* Arlington, VA: Council for Exceptional Children.

Baker, S. B., & Gerler, E. R., Jr. (2008). *School counseling for the twenty-first century* (5th ed.). Upper Saddle River, NJ: Pearson.

Batsche, G., Elliot, J., Graden, J. L., Grimes, J., Kovaleski, J. F., & Prasse, D. (2005). *Response to intervention: Policy Considerations and Implementation.* Alexandria, VA: NASDSE.

Bauman, S. (2008). The role of elementary school counselors in reducing school bullying. *The Elementary School Journal, 108*, 362–375. doi:10.1086/589467

Baumberger, J. P., & Harper, R. E. (2007). *Assisting students with disabilities: A handbook for school counselors* (2nd ed.). Thousand Oaks, CA: Corwin Press.

Bd. of Educ. of Hendrick Hudson v. Rowley, 458 U.S. 1976 (1982).

Benfer, E. A. (2009, September). *The ADA Amendments Act: An overview of recent changes to the Americans with Disabilities Act.* Washington, DC: American Constitution Society for Law and Policy. Retrieved from http://www.acslaw.org/files/Benfer%20ADAAA_0.pdf

Board of Education of Cleveland Heights v. State ex rel. Goldman, 47 Ohio App. 417, 191 N.E. 914 (1934).

Bowen, M. L., & Glenn, E. (1998). Counseling interventions for students who have mild disabilities. *Professional School Counseling, 2*, 16–25. Retrieved from http://www.questia.com/PM.qst?a=o&d=5035383445

Bradley, C. (1956). Interdisciplinary teamwork in special education. *Exceptional Children, 23*, 5–38.

Bradley, D. F., King-Sears, M. E., & Tessier-Switlick, D. M. (1997). *Teaching students in inclusive settings from theory to practice.* Boston, MA: Allyn & Bacon.

Brown v. Board of Education, 37 U.S. 483 (1954).

Buck v. Bell, 274 U.S. 200 (1927).

Campbell, C. A., & Dahir, C. A. (1997). *Sharing the vision: The national standards for school counseling programs.* Alexandria, VA: American School Counselor Association.

Carter, E. W., Clark, N. M., Cushing, L. S., & Kennedy, C. H. (2005). Moving from elementary to middle school: Supporting a smooth transition for students with severe disabilities. *TEACHING Exceptional Children, 37*(3), 8-14.

Center on Response to Intention. (n.d.). *The essential components of RTI.* http://www.rti4success.org/

Chata, C. C., & Loesch, L. C. (2007). Future school principals' views of the roles of professional school counselors. *Professional School Counseling, 11,* 35–41. doi:10.5330/PSC.n.2010-11.35

Clark, M. A., & Breman, J. C. (2009). School counselor inclusion: A collaborative model to provide academic and social-emotional support in the classroom setting. *Journal of Counseling and Development, 87,* 6-11.

The College Board. (n.d.). *Recommendations: Counselor tips.* Retrieved from http://professionals.collegeboard.com/guidance/applications/counselor-tips

Corey, M., & Corey, G. (2002). *Groups: Process and practice* (6th ed.). Pacific Grove, CA: Brooks/Cole.

Council for Exceptional Children. (2010). *Individuals With Disabilities Education Act 2004.* Alexandria, VA: Author. Retrieved from http://www.cec.sped.org/AM/Template.cfm?Section=IDEA_2004&Template=/TaggedPage/TaggedPageDisplay.cfm&TPLID=9&ContentID=3533

Council for the Accreditation of Counseling and Related Educational Programs. (2009). *CACREP 2009 standards.* Alexandria, VA: Author. Retrieved from http://www.cacrep.org/doc/2009%20Standards%20with%20cover.pdf

Dorr, G. M. (2010, February 24). *Buck v. Bell (1927)*. Retrieved from Encyclopedia Virginia: http://www.EncyclopediaVirginia.org/Buck_v_Bell_1927

Education for All Handicapped Children Act of 1975, Pub. L. 94-142, 89 Stat. 773 (20 U.S.C. § 1400 *et seq.*) (1975).

The Education Trust. (1997). *The national guidance and counseling reform program*. Washington, DC: Author.

Elementary and Secondary Education Act of 1965, Pub. L. 89–10, *as added* Pub. L. 103-382, 108 Stat. 3519 (20 U.S.C. § 6301 *et seq.*) (1965)

Erford, B. T. (2007). *Transforming the school counseling profession* (2nd ed.). Upper Saddle River, NJ: Pearson.

Estell, D. B., Farmer, T. W., Irvin, M. J., Crowther, A., Akos, P., & Boudah, D. J. (2009). Students with exceptionalities and the peer group context of bullying and victimization in late elementary school. *Journal of Child and Family Studies, 18*, 136–150.

Family Educational Rights and Privacy Act of 1974, 20 U.S.C. § 1232g (2006).

FERPA Regulations, 34 CFR § 99.31 (2009).

Foster, S., Rolefson, M., Doksum, T., Noonan, D., Robinson, G., & Teich, J. (2005). *School mental health services in the United States 2002-2003*. DHHS Pub. No. (SMA) 05-4068. Rockville, MD: Center for Mental Health Services, Substance Abuse and Mental Health Services Administration. Retrieved from http://www.eric.ed.gov:80/PDFS/ED499056.pdf

Foundation for Child Development. (2010). *Child and youth well-being index (CWI)*. New York, NY: Author. Retrieved from http://www.fcd-us.org/sites/default/files/FINAL%202010%20CWI%20Annual%20Release.pdf

Frasier, J. R. (2007). Transitioning students with disabilities from middle to high school. *TEACHING Exceptional Children Plus, 4*(2), 2–10.

Glossoff, H. L., & Pate, R. H., Jr. (2002). Privacy and confidentiality in school counseling. *Professional School Counseling, 6*, 20–27.

Greer, B. B., Greer, J. G., & Woody, D. E. (1995). The inclusion movement and its impact on counselors. *The School Counselor, 43*, 124–132.

Hallahan, D. P., & Kauffman, J. M. (2006). *Exceptional learners: An introduction to special education* (10th ed.). Boston, MA: Allyn & Bacon.

Honig v. Doe, 484 U.S. 305 (1988).

Horner, R. H. & Sugai, G. (2000). School-wide behavior support: An emerging initiative (Special issue). *Journal of Positive Behavioral Interventions, 2,* 231–232.

House, R. M., & Hayes, R. L. (2002). School counselors: Becoming key players in school reform. *Professional School Counseling, 5,* 249–256.

IDEA Regulations, 34 C.F.R. § 300 (2006).

Individuals with Disabilities Education Act, 20 U.S.C. ¶ 4301 *et seq.* (2006)

Irving Independent Sch. Dist. v. Amber Tatro, 468 U.S. 883 (1984).

Jorgensen, M. A., & Hoffmann, J. (2003). *History of the No Child Left Behind Act of 2001 (NCLB)*; (Rev.). Upper Saddle River, NJ: Pearson. Retrieved from http://www.pearsonassessments.com/NR/rdonlyres/ D8E33AAE-BED1-4743-98A1-BDF4D49D7274/0/HistoryofNCLB_ Rev2_Final.pdf

Kirk, S., Gallagher, J. J., Coleman, M. R., & Anastasiow, N. (2009). *Educating exceptional children* (10th ed.). Boston, MA: Houghton Mifflin Harcourt.

Lambie, G. W., & Williamson, L. L. (2004). The challenge to change from guidance counseling to professional school counseling: A historical proposition. *Professional School Counseling, 8,* 124–131.

Larkin, C., & Callaghan, P. (2005). Professionals' perceptions of interprofessional working in community mental health teams. *Journal of Interprofessional Care, 19,* 338–346. doi:10.1080/13561820500165282

Madaus, J. W., & Shaw, S. F. (2008). The role of school professionals in implementing Section 504 for students with disabilities. *Educational Policy, 22,* 363–378. doi:10.1177/0895904807307069

Mastropieri, M. A., & Scruggs, T. E. (2004). *The inclusive classroom: Strategies for effective instruction* (2nd ed.). Upper Saddle River, NJ: Prentice Hall.

McEachern, A. G. (2003). School counselor preparation to meet the guidance needs of exceptional students: A national study. *Counselor Education and Supervision, 42,* 314–325.

McNeil, M. (2009, July 23). Race to Top guidelines stress use of test data. *Education Week.* Retrieved http://www.edweek.org/ew/articles/2009/07/23/37race.h28.html

Mellard, D. F., Byrd, S. E., Johnson, E., Tollefson, J. M., & Boesche, L. (2004). Foundations and research on identifying model responsiveness-to-intervention sites. *Learning Disability Quarterly, 27,* 243-256. doi:10.2307/1593676

Merikangas, K. R., He, J., Burstein, M., Swanson, S. A., Avenevoli, S., Cui, L., . . . Swendsen, J. (2010). Lifetime prevalence of mental disorders in U.S. adolescents: Results from the National Comorbidity Survey Replication-Adolescent Supplement (NCS-A). *Journal of the American Academy of Child & Adolescent Psychiatry,* (49, 980–989. doi:10.1016/j.jaac.2010.05.017

Michan, S. M., & Rodger, S. A. (2005). Effective health care teams: A model of six characteristics developed from shared perceptions. *Journal of Interprofessional Care, 19,* 358–370. doi:10.1080/13561820500165142

Mills v. Board of Education of the District of Columbia, 348 F. Supp. 866 (D. DC 1972).

Milsom, A. (2007). Interventions to assist students with disabilities through school transitions. *Professional School Counseling, 10,* 273–278.

Milsom, A., & Dietz, L. (2009). Defining college readiness for students with learning disabilities: A Delphi study. *Professional School Counseling, 12,* 315–323. doi:10.5330/PSC.n.2010-12.315

Milsom, A., & Hartley, M. A. (2005). Assisting students with learning disabilities transitioning to college: What school counselors should know. *Professional School Counseling, 8,* 436–441.

Milsom, A. S. (2002). Students with disabilities: School counselor involvement and preparation. *Professional School Counseling, 5,* 331–338.

Mishna, F. (2003). Learning disabilities and bullying: Double jeopardy. *Journal of Learning Disabilities, 36,* 336–347. doi:10.1177/00222194030360040501

Mizelle, N. B., & Irvin, J. L. (2000). Transition from middle school into high school. *Middle School Journal, 31,* 57–61.

Musheno, S., & Talbert, M. (2002). The transformed school counselor in action. *Theory Into Practice, 41*, 186–191. doi:10.1207/s15430421tip4103_7

National Career Development Association. (2004). *National career development guidelines* (Rev.). Broken Arrow, OK: Author.

National Center for Education Statistics. (2010). *Digest of education statistics, 2009* (NCES 2010-013), *Chapter 2*. Washington, DC: U.S. Department of Education. Retrieved from http://nces.ed.gov/fastfacts/display. asp?id=64

National Center for Learning Disabilities. (2009). Understanding the Americans With Disabiltiies Act Amendments Act and Section 504 of the Rehabilitation Act: The impact on students with LD and AD/HD (Parent Advocacy Brief). New York, NY: Author. Retrieved from http://www.ncld.org/ images/stories/Publications/AdvocacyBriefs/UnderstandingADAAA-Section504/UnderstandingADAAA-Section504.pdf

National Center on Response to Intervention. (2010, April). *Essential components of RTI – a closer look at response to intervention.* Washington, DC: Author. Retrieved from http://www.rti4success.org/images/stories/ pdfs/rtiessentialcomponents_051310.pdf

National Council on Disability. (2000, January). *Back to school on civil rights.* Retrieved from http://www.ncd.gov/newsroom/publications/2000/ backtoschool_1.htm

National Education Association. (2007). *Truth in labeling: Disproportionality in special education.* Washington, DC: Author. Retrieved from http:// www.nccrest.org/Exemplars/Disporportionality_Truth_In_Labeling.pdf

No Child Left Behind Act of 2001, 20 U.S.C. § 6301 *et seq.* (2006)

Novosel, L. C., & Deshler, D. C. (2010). Response to intervention. In R. T. Boon & V. Spencer (Eds.), *Best practices for the inclusive classroom: An evidence-based guide for teachers* (pp. 1–24). Waco, TX: Prufrock.

Oberti v. Bd. of Educ. of Borough of Clementon Sch. Dist., 789 F.Supp, 1322 (D.N.J. 1992).

Office of Civil Rights. (2010). *Protecting students with disabilities: Frequently asked questions about Section 504 and the education of children with disabilities.* Retrieved from http://www2.ed.gov/print/about/offices/list/ ocr/504faq.html

Office of Special Education Programs. (n.d.-a). *Positive behavioral supports and the law.* http://www.pbis.org/school/pbis_and_the_law/default.aspx

Office of Special Education Programs. (n.d.-b). *Response to Intervention (RTI) & PBIS.* Retrieved from www.pbis.org/school/rti.aspx

Office of Special Education Programs. (n.d.-b). *School-wide PBIS.* Retrieved from http://www.pbis.org/school/default.aspx

Paulsen, K. J. (2010). Collaboration. In R. T. Boon & V. G. Spencer (Eds.), *Best practices for the inclusive classroom: An evidence-based guide for teachers* (pp. 87–109). Waco, TX: Profrock Press.

Pearce, L. R. (2009). Helping children with emotional difficulties: a response to intervention investigation. *The Rural Educator, 30*(2), 34–46.

Penn. Assoc. for Retarded Children (PARC) v. Commonwealth of Pennsylvania, 334 F.Supp. 1257 (E.D Pa. 1972).

Pérusse, R., Goodnough, G. E., Donegan, J., & Jones, C. (2004). Perceptions of school counselors and school principals about the National Standards for School Counseling Programs and the Transforming School Counseling Initiative. *Professional School Counseling, 7,* 152–161.

Regan, K. S. (2009). Improving the way we think about students with emotional and/or behavioral disorders. *TEACHING Exceptional Children, 41*(5), 60–65.

Rehabilitation Act of 1973, Pub. L. 93-112, 87 Stat. 355 (29 U.S.C. 701 *et seq.*). (1973).

Rock, E., & Leff, E. H. (2007). The professional school counselor and students with disabilities. In B. T. Erford (Ed.), *Transforming the school counseling profession* (pp. 318–350). Upper Saddle River, NJ: Pearson.

Romano, J. L., & Kachgal, M. M. (2004). Counseling psychology and school counseling: An underutilized partnership. *The Counseling Psychologist, 32,* 184–215. doi:10.1177/0011000003261354

Santos de Barona, M., & Barona, A. (2006). School counselors and school psychologists: Collaborating to ensure minority students receive appropriate consideration for special educational programs. *Professional School Counseling, 10,* 3–13.

Savickas, M. (2009). Pioneers of the vocational guidance movement: A centennial celebration. *The Career Development Quarterly, 57*, 194–198.

Scarborough, J. L., & Gilbride, D. D. (2006). Developing relationships with rehabilitation counselors to meet the transition needs of students with disabilities. *Professional School Counseling, 10*, 25–33.

Schaffer v. Weast, (04-698) 546 U.S. 49 (2005) 377 F.3d 449, *affirmed.*

Schoen, S., & Schoen, A. (2010). Bullying and harassment in the United States. *The Clearing House: A Journal of Educational Strategies, Issues and Ideas, 83*(2), 68–72.

Schulting, A. B., Malone, P. S., & Dodge, K. A. (2006). The effect of school-based kindergarten transition policies and practices on child academic outcomes. *Developmental Psychology, 41*, 860–871. doi:10.1037/0012-1649.41.6.860

Sheard, A. G., & Kakabadse, A. P. (2002). From loose groups to effective teams. *Journal of Management Development, 21*, 133–151. doi:10.1108/02621710210417439

Stone, C. (2004, March 1). *The legal and ethical complications in letters of recommendation.* American School Counselor Association. Retrieved from http://www.schoolcounselor.org/article.asp?article=753&paper=91&cat=140

Taub, D. J. (2006). Understanding the concerns of parents of students with disabilities: Challenges and roles for school counselors. *Professional School Counseling, 10*, 51–57

Trussell, R. T. (2008). Classroom universals to prevent problem behaviors. *Intervention in School and Clinic, 43*, 179–185. doi:10.1177/1053451207311678

Tuckman, B. W. (1965). Development sequences in small groups. *Psychology Bulletin, 63*, 384–399. doi:10.1037/h0022100

U.S Department of Education. (2010). *The condition of education 2010* (NCES 2010-028). Washington, DC: Author. Retrieved from http://nces.ed.gov/pubs2010/2010028.pdf

U.S. Department of Health and Human Services. (2000). *U.S. Surgeon General's report on children's mental health.* Washington, DC: Author.

Virginia Department of Education. (2009, April). *RtI Response to intervention: RtI and the special education eligibility process. Frequently asked questions.* Retrieved from http://www.doe.virginia.gov/instruction/response_intervention/guidance/special_ed_eligibility_faq.pdf

Wagner, M., Newman, L., & Cameto, R. (2004, April). *Changes over time in the secondary school experiences of students with disabilities. A report of findings from the National Longitudinal Transition Study (NLTS) and the National Longitudinal Transition Study-2 (NLTS2).* Menlo Park, CA: SRI International. Retrieved from http://www.eric.ed.gov:80/PDFS/ED494937.pdf

Wrenn, C. G. (1962). *The counselor in a changing world.* Washington, DC: American Personnel and Guidance Association.

Yell, M. L., Rogers, D., & Rogers, E. L. (1998). The legal history of special education: What a long, strange trip it's been! *Remedial and Special Education, 19,* 219–228. doi:10.1177/074193259801900405

Yell, M. L., Shriner, J. G. & Katsiyannis, A. (2006). Individuals with Disabilities Education Improvement Act of 2004 and IDEA Regulations of 2006: Implications for educators, administrators, and teacher trainers. *Focus on Exceptional Children, 39,* 1–24.

Zhang, D., & Katsiyannis, A. (2002). Minority representation in special education: A persistent challenge. *Remedial and Special Education, 23,* 180–187. doi:10.1177/07419325020230030601

Zigmond, N. (2003). Where should students with disabilities receive special education services? Is one place better than another? *The Journal of Special Education, 37,* 193–198. doi:10.1177/00224669030370030901

Zirkel, P. A. (2009). What does the law say? New Section 504 student eligibility standards. *TEACHING Exceptional Children, 41*(4), 68–71.

End

what
School Counselors
Need to Know

About Special Education and Students With Disabilities

Revised Edition

Barbara E. Baditoi, Ed.D.

Pamelia E. Brott, Ph.D., NCC

Council for
Exceptional
Children
The voice and vision of special education

Council for Exceptional Children
2900 Crystal Drive, Suite 1000
Arlington, VA 22202
www.cec.sped.org

Printed in the United States of America by AGS

Library of Congress Cataloging-in-Publication data
Baditoi, Barbara E.
What school counselors need to know about special education and students with
disabilities / by Barbara E. Baditoi and Pamelia E. Brott
p. cm.
Includes biographical references

ISBN 978-0-86586-501-3 (soft cover edition)
ISBN 978-0-86586-503-7 (eBook edition)

First edition revised
10 9 8 7 6 5 4 3 2 1

Acknowledgments

This book was born out of respect for the work of school counselors and the professional and caring manner in which they practice. It is written with thanks on behalf of special education students who benefit from the positive and proactive manner in which school counselors meet their needs.

The idea for the book came from a collaborative effort between a Counselor Education Program university faculty member and a Director of Special Education and Student Services to promote best practices in the fields of special education and school counseling. Both authors saw the need for a resource that can be used both in training future school counselors and by school counselors in the field. The purpose of the book is to bring together information, suggestions, forms, and resources so that school counselors can meet the needs of general and special education students and staff in our schools.

The authors would like to express their sincerest appreciation to the professional school counselors and administrators who took the time to review the manuscript and provide helpful suggestions to make this book a reality. Thanks to Janet Kremer, Marcia Schumann, Janae Rittenhouse, Elise Kenney, Suzanne Davidson, Dr. Betty Riordan, Dr. Ann McCarty, and Dr. David Czarnecki for your reviews, ideas, and insightful recommendations and contributions to our overall work.

In addition, we would like to thank the Council for Exceptional Children for believing in our idea and supporting our wanderings as we merged the fields of school counseling and special education. Lorraine Sobson, copyediting for the first edition and CEC Publications Manager for the revised edition, is owed a debt of gratitude for listening to our questions and comments and never second guessing our intent.